CLEARING

Photo © Sarah O'Brien

About the Author

Alexandra Chauran is a second-generation fortuneteller and a professional psychic intuitive. For more than a decade, she has served thousands of clients in the Seattle area and globally through her website. She is certified in tarot and has been interviewed on National Public Radio and other major media outlets. Alexandra is currently pursuing a doctoral degree, lives in Issaquah, Washington, and can be found online at EarthShod.com.

To Write the Author

If you wish to contact the author or would like more information about this book, please write to the author in care of Llewellyn Worldwide, and we will forward your request. Both the author and publisher appreciate hearing from you and learning of your enjoyment of this book and how it has helped you. Llewellyn Worldwide cannot guarantee that every letter written to the author can be answered, but all will be forwarded. Please write to:

Alexandra Chauran
℅ Llewellyn Worldwide
2143 Wooddale Drive
Woodbury, MN 55125-2989

Please enclose a self-addressed stamped envelope for reply,
or $1.00 to cover costs. If outside the USA, enclose
an international postal reply coupon.

Alexandra Chauran

CLEARING CLUTTER

Physical   Mental   Spiritual

Llewellyn Publications
Woodbury, Minnesota

FIRST EDITION
First Printing, 2015

Book design by Bob Gaul
Cover art by iStockphoto.com/22781818/©stocknroll
Cover design by Lisa Novak
Editing by Laura Graves
Interior flowers from *Flowers Vector Designs* © 2010 Dover Publications, Inc.

Llewellyn Publications is a registered trademark of Llewellyn Worldwide Ltd.

Library of Congress Cataloging-in-Publication Data
Chauran, Alexandra, 1981–
    Clearing clutter: physical, mental, spiritual/Alexandra Chauran—First Edition.
        pages cm
    Includes bibliographical references.
    ISBN 978-0-7387-4227-4
    1. Orderliness. I. Title.
    BJ1533.O73C43 2015
    131—dc23
                                    2015009107

Llewellyn Publications
A Division of Llewellyn Worldwide Ltd.
2143 Wooddale Drive
Woodbury, MN 55125-2989
www.llewellyn.com

Printed in the United States of America

Contents

"The simplified life is a sanctified life, much more calm, much less strife. Oh, what wondrous truths are unveiled—Projects succeed which had previously failed. Oh, how beautiful life can be, Beautiful simplicity."

....

Peace Pilgrim

Introduction

I grew up in a cluttered home. My dad was a collector by nature and identity, and our home was nicely lived-in, with strange objects from travels and adventure poking out from every shelf and corner, his quirky touch everywhere. My mother's paintings and carvings of Egyptian deities peered loftily from the walls and mantle. Pirate's doubloons littered the hallway. Dad had stamps from exotic nations and military medals that were always displayed alongside photos of the recipients. One could see the stories of heroes shining in their eyes. Our surroundings were hardly the spectacle of hoarders. To me, what we had felt like home—the accumulated achievements of a family who valued travel and its associated tales of adventure.

The dusty belongings weren't half of the clutter, however. Even our schedules were cluttered. Between choir practice, scouts, organized weekend group hikes, homework, and academic games, there was little time left for friendships and spirituality for any member of our family. This frenetic pace was embraced and encouraged. Even though we were not poor by any means, my father managed finances the way a rock-climber seeks the next big thrill. Last-minute bill paying and budgeting down to the dime were the norm. The inner message was that there was no room for error. No room, indeed, because everything was accounted for and our cups ran over with blessings and responsibilities.

My mother would later call this time of her life her "years of rice and salt." She was paying her dues, waiting for the time when she could be retired with an open schedule and a condo furnished with minimalist IKEA furniture. It's odd to me still to think that these were hard times for her. To me they were the warm and nourishing days of childhood. The clutter formed the background noise that came to feel comfortable and safe for me. I didn't even notice that both my aunt and the mother of my best friend were hoarders, stuffing their homes and lives with belongings to disastrous effect.

When I became an adult and moved in with my husband, our merged belongings represented two lifetimes of adventure that had collided. As a young newlywed, however, I was not content with my life. My husband and I consulted with a marriage and family therapist, and were counseled on all of the challenges one would expect of a couple going through a quarter-life crisis. I confided in the counselor my hopes, dreams, and fears for the future: I wanted children, I was dissatisfied with my career and physical fitness, and both of us were disappointed with our home.

It was at that moment in the warm lighting of the therapist's office that she said something to us, a revelation, that also struck me as obvious: every individual feels dissatisfied with life experience. Every life deviates from original "plans." No matter how close to my goals I could get, I would still lack contentment unless I found what was truly missing. Because if at length that piece is found, then theoretically I wouldn't have any need for the rest of my desires. In other words, sometimes you only get what you want when you stop needing it so desperately.

I'd like to tell you that I got up from that therapist's couch, wiped the tears from my eyes, and promptly cleared up all the clutter in my life that instant. Alas, it took me years to fully understand that spirituality was the creamy center lacking in my life. And during that same period I had to begin the hard work of clearing space in my life, a concept that would have been quite foreign to me during my upbringing. It wasn't easy, and when I see friends and family struggling with clutter I feel the utmost empathy for their struggles. I'm not saying that you must be religious to fill your life; that may seem too simple or too complex. However, I am saying that you need to become a seeker for that which truly matters and what is truly missing from this life that you have been so far stuffing with clutter.

This book will give you a way to start immediately defining and dealing with your life's clutter and discover what "clutter" means to you on a deeper level. We'll go through clearing physical and mental clutter first, starting with the material form of clutter if you are feeling buried and overwhelmed with it in your physical space. Then, we'll tackle the clutter as it affects your spirit. In this book, "spiritual" refers to any sort of deeper meaning or purpose in your life, which may include a relationship with higher powers. Connection with the universe is a thread woven throughout this book. We'll find the center of simplicity in your life to which you can return, rather than resume your cluttering ways. Finally, I'll address problem of helping others clear clutter, for those of you who may be tasked with helping a loved one who has a cluttered life or who has bequeathed a large amount of clutter to you after a life event.

Since the concepts in this book build on one another, I recommend reading the chapters in order, even if some of the different forms of clutter I've described don't quite apply. If you're not a very spiritual person or if your mental life isn't cluttered right now, the related clearing methods may seem like trying to put out a house fire with a teacup, but the concepts do meld together when carefully applied in the proper order. Think of the three aspects of clutter: physical, mental, spiritual, as sides of a balanced triangle. One cannot cherry pick parts of the book to use—it's all about balance between the three. That said, you may wish to read this book with a highlighter or a stack of sticky notes at hand. Make note of the tips that will be most helpful to you; the ones you want to focus on and put into practice.

Are you prepared? The road ahead will present many obstacles. You may have to confront and tackle some inner demons that have been hiding among the clutter. If what follows was as simple as cleaning a room, most of us would have already met with success. You can do this and keep your mind, body, and spirit intact during the process.

"In my life, what I want and what
I need are exactly the same. Anything
in excess of needs is burdensome to me."

....

Peace Pilgrim

One

············

Getting Started:
What Is Clutter?

As you start this chapter, your first step won't be to put on your cleaning gloves or to get out the donation bags. Instead, it will be to examine the problem from all angles, some of which may require inner work.

There is a Buddhist story about a monk who returned to his small cottage after a long walk in the woods because it had started to rain. When he opened the door, he was shocked to find that his cottage was in a shambles because of the wind blowing through the open windows. The books and writings on his desk were scattered all over the floor and his bed. Worst of all, his important documents were still swirling in the moist, stormy air, making it impossible for him to chase them down and pick them up to place them back in order.

The wise monk, knowing what to do, left the papers to fly and first went to shutter each of the open windows and to seal the door. Only when the wind was no longer pushing all of his precious belongings up against the walls and his furniture was he able to begin carefully picking up his small cottage.

Of course, the above story is a metaphor. The cottage represents the mind, and when the monk closed the windows and door, he was actually telling the story listener to close his eyes and sit still in meditation in order to quiet the mind and bring order to his thoughts. In this story, the physical clutter of a living space, the mental clutter of a harried mind, and the spiritual clutter of a life whose purpose has been thrown off track come together. I use this parable to illustrate the true nature of clutter, which is any impediment to the proper flow of energy.

What Is Energy?

When I use the word "energy" in this book, I do not mean the literal and scientific definition bound to electrical, chemical, thermal, or other work. Rather, energy in this context represents the universal substance with which our thoughts and goals are made manifest. This metaphorical, spiritual energy is called *chi* in Eastern religions, and is thought by many to be the life force that flows within each of us and through our environs. I use the term "energy" because it is a metaphor for the more familiar definition of the word, in that people need it in order to perform work. It is also like the colloquial use of the term in that if your energy is too low, you may be unable to do much of anything, but if your energy is too high your activity may be frenetic and anxious. Thus, energy can be a positive or a negative influence due to its flow. For now, think of the negative influence of energy as the wind blowing through that monk's cottage, cluttering his mind.

Clutter as Myth and Metaphor

You may have already noticed that I believe clutter to be deeper and more significant in one's life than just a pile of clean but unfolded laundry. Throughout this book, I want you to keep in mind the monk's cottage and the metaphor of life energy that can be impeded when it runs up against the pile of unopened junk mail on your coffee table or the unfinished projects on your desk. Clutter is also the constant chattering in your mind that ruminates on past mistakes or worries about the future. Even your spiritual life can become cluttered with disappointment or expectations about your place in the universe and your relationship with spirit.

Small stray objects can seem larger as representing clutter as part of the big picture. I've noticed, for example, that I simply cannot abide clutter on my coffee table. Please don't imagine that my house is squeaky clean, however; I have pets and young children. The same objects that can collect happily on a shelf or accumulate in a drawer make me feel overwhelmed if I see them on the wide expanse the coffee table. To me, the coffee table has become more than a cheap piece of furniture rescued from a sale. It is a stage on which my kids can dance or parade new clothes. It is the empty canvas of my precious recreational time, just ready to be painted with a puzzle or a new craft to learn. It is the tableau around which my household turns, representing our family's coming and going.

When clutter appears on the coffee table or somewhere else that is of special psychological importance, my husband and I joke that it "scratches my aura," meaning that it affects my energy level and mood in a negative way. In this way, physical clutter can be more than just something that can trip you up in life in a literal way, it can hobble you on other levels of mind, body, and spirit.

Different Types of Clutter

In 1953, a 45-year-old woman named Mildred Ryder had a spiritual awakening and saw that the world had too much clutter in body, mind, and spirit. She believed she knew steps toward inner peace that people could use to relinquish their attachments to things, relationships, and even thoughts. She divested herself of her possessions except for a simple blue outfit and a pair of good shoes. She made a solemn vow to herself: "I shall not accept more than I need while others in the world have less than they need." Then she left her home and spent the next twenty-eight years of her life walking more than 25,000 miles around the United States, trying to bring her message of peace and clarity of purpose to the world. She even left behind her old name and chose to call herself the Peace Pilgrim.

This remarkable woman made a life-changing vow to remain a wanderer, but I'm certainly not advocating that. However, I will be sharing some of her teachings, as well as the teachings of many others with you throughout this book because Peace believed in simplicity. She believed, as I do, that clutter can weigh down the spirit. It can affect your life and the lives of everyone within your sphere of influence.

Have you ever been so filled with so much stress and busy thinking that you have been completely unable to settle down to perform even the most routine household tasks like doing dishes or laundry? If so, you already understand that mental clutter directly affects physical clutter. In fact, I will go a step further and say that if you are unable to unclutter your mind, you will be unable to keep your home clutter-free as well, because the two types of energy flow problems interact to form a larger problem.

There is a third and more elusive type of clutter, that of the spirit. In this book, the spiritual refers to finding any sort of deeper meaning or purpose in your life, which may include a relationship with higher powers. We'll get to the heart of the matter by addressing the realm of spirit as it pertains to spiritual confusion. Spiritual confusion relates to clutter because our lives are busy with so many other things that we feel disconnected from spirit, or we are abiding by what others have said what to believe instead of what we feel, think, and connect with on a spiritual level. Different people are born with different hungers for spirit. Some are spiritual at a very young age, while others develop that hunger later in life. Many people develop a serious problem with clutter when they are middle aged or older, which seems to coincide with their spiritual hunger, whether consciously or subconsciously. As one of my spiritual teachers used to say, "there are no coincidences."

Clutter is brought into our minds, homes, and other spaces to try to fill the void left by a lack of spiritual fulfillment. But here's the truth: nothing else can fill that hole. No cherished collections, status symbols, books, or academic degrees can do it—not even family and monetary success. Paradoxically, the spiritually enlightened person will seem to be content with having nothing. I'm not going to try to convince you to shave your head and give away all your possessions, but I will push you to begin to seek balance and work on the clutter in your mind, body and spirit. This might push you out of your comfort zone, especially if you've never perceived yourself as a spiritually hungry person.

Doubt is a good thing. It will either bring you back to believe in your own present philosophy stronger than ever, or it will help lead you to something better.

The Nature of the Beast

Here's a silly conversation I had with my husband. I had just given birth to my second child, so I was unable to do as much of the maintenance housework as usual. Luckily, I was blessed with his help and the assistance of my best friend. While I was nursing the baby and my friend cared for my eldest, I asked my husband to sweep the floor, as it looked rather dirty. He looked at me as if I was crazy. "But I just swept it yesterday," he said. "If I sweep it now, it will just get dirty again!" I had to laugh; he had stumbled upon a basic truth about cleaning and clearing clutter.

Clearing clutter is a constant activity, a lifestyle rather than a one-time intervention that solves a problem. Even the most admirably clutter-free people are only so successful because they have learned how to keep up with the flow of clutter in and out of life. They might hire a maid for their house, but can they hire one for their brain or their heart? Embrace the cliché that life is about the journey, not the destination. The reality is that you can't relax forever into cleared space any more than you can relax forever without material obligations such as earning and spending money. Instead, learn to dance in the space you have and find joy in the process of clearing space for future happiness.

Attachments

I was a bit dubious when I first heard there were some spiritual people out there who worked to relinquish attachments. I love people in my life and I love stuff. To me, it seemed like there was absolutely nothing spiritual about throwing away perfectly useful things or people. However, it turned out that I was misunderstanding the nature of attachment. One can still enjoy relationships with people and ownership of plenty of possessions without establishing unnecessary attachments.

The word "attachment" may be problematic because it may create associations with the perfectly natural psychological word for creating an attachment to people in life. In the discipline of psychology, a healthy attachment with caregivers is the first important thing that an infant gains in life. In psychology, an attachment is what first creates a sense of trust and faith in the world. Without a healthy attachment in infancy, a person may grow up without the ability to form healthy relationships. However, in a spiritual context, unnecessary attachments are unhealthy.

Unhealthy attachment in a relationships entails a sense of ownership. When a person is too attached to someone else, they may tend to micromanage the person or the relationship. The other person might feel stifled or smothered. Too much attachment may even drive others away. Conversely, releasing a sense of ownership and clinging instead to faith and trust can enhance the relationship. Without being overly attached, both people can feel the freedom to pursue hobbies and goals without feeling chained to a controlling partner. Ideally, both people could pursue independent goals and freely check in with each other as needed. Incidentally, this reflects the healthy form of psychological attachment in which an infant will explore away from a parent and check in with him or her on occasion.

Attachment to objects is not a vital part of human psychology and it can become both mentally and spiritually problematic. This doesn't mean that you have to give up everything and live an austere life. Instead of focusing on how strongly you are attached to objects, think about how much those objects may trap you or prevent energy in your life from flowing freely. If the objects in your life are useful and used frequently in your hobbies, for example, things are working well. If the objects in your life are interfering with your plans to move because they are tethering you to your job or your present living space, however, you may be dealing with too much attachment.

Letting Go of Negativity

You can get rid of old and negative thoughts by catching yourself in the act and replacing them with new, positive scripts. With your meditation and prayer skills and mantras (detailed in chapter 3), you can take these activities to a new level. Instead of waiting around for negativity to happen to you, you can ward it off. Visualize what you want to have happen in your life and cling to that vision. Now, you have the skills to let go of attachments as soon as they become unnecessary. Think of avoiding negativity as if you were Tarzan swinging through vines in the jungle. Grab hold of your goals only so long as they serve you. When you are ready to move forward, let go and progress without letting yourself fall behind or repeat the past.

Go Easy on Yourself

Given that clutter clearing is an ongoing process, you'll need to cut yourself some slack, especially if you've let things get out of hand. For me, cleaning the house from top to bottom only makes it less likely that I will want to put my hand on the door of the closet of cleaning supplies the next day. You'll have to cut your work into reasonably sized chunks to keep your motivation and morale high. Metaphorically, the same is also true with less tangible forms of clutter when reforming your intellectual and spiritual life. A true lifestyle change doesn't have to be a shock to your system. In fact, it is better if you can avoid it.

If you do feel like you need a massive overhaul in your life, first assess your resources for coping. Resources for coping can be physical, such as good health, the helping hands of friends and family, or financial support. Resources for coping can also be mental and spiritual, such as a sense of resilience in the face of adversity and your faith in a positive outcome. If you have plenty of resources for coping at your disposal, feel free to make more drastic changes in your life. If your resources for coping are limited, however, you'll need to stick with baby steps.

....

Clearing-Clutter Tip: Take photographs along your clearing-clutter journey. Just like physical fitness after weight loss, clearing clutter is a lifestyle change as well as a long-term goal.

You're not going to see habits change overnight. Keeping a record will help you see progress over time, even if you sometimes take some backward steps.

....

Degrees of Clutter

There are varying degrees of clutter in life requiring different approaches. I'll give you a few examples in the different realms of mind, body, and spirit so that you can get a sense about what each clutter problem looks like. Keep in mind that you might need the help of a trusted loved one to help you assess your own degrees of clutter. Like a fish swimming in water, it may be difficult to notice something that surrounds you. Conversely, your own sense of responsibility might cause you to unfairly compare yourself to others in a way that grossly overestimates your own clutter. I'm sure that you've been to somebody's house where the host says, "Oh, I'm so sorry for the mess," and you wondered what in the world she was talking about, as her home was spotless compared to yours! Just remember, no matter how bad your clutter problem may be, there's always somebody worse off. Also, clearing clutter is an ongoing process. Those who have admirably cleared their lives of clutter are always working to do so, just like you.

Physical Clutter

Physical clutter includes household clutter, a messy office or desk, a car filled with garbage and dirt, and an unweeded garden. Physical clutter may also include "body clutter," which is a body whose basic health such as nutrition, exercise, and sleep are being neglected to the point that a person is underweight, overweight, or exhausted.

Low-level maintenance needs

If clutter is at a low level, your physical space is constantly churning through problems as they arise. For example, your home may be generally uncluttered, though messy areas or "hot spots" might accumulate when bills are due or when guests arrive. Low-level metaphorical clutter in the body looks like a generally healthy lifestyle with occasional lapses in diet or exercise that require serious concentration for brief periods of time without resulting in low self-esteem. At this degree of clutter, you might not be embarrassed to invite people over to your home and you would be able to quickly find items that you need in your office.

Moderate overwhelm

Moderate overwhelm typically occurs because of a transient life issue that hampers your ability to cope, such as moving house, having a newborn baby or suffering an injury. At this level, embarrassment or shame is a key emotion when people come over and see that the normal processes of your home seem to have been backed up or stopped entirely. Dishes may pile up in the sink and laundry becomes a losing battle. The floors of your home and your bathrooms gather filth at an alarming rate. With moderate overwhelm you may feel constantly just behind your goals, which increases your problem with motivation. Moderate body clutter looks like somebody who struggles with yo-yo dieting or who has fallen into a sedentary lifestyle. It may be appropriate to be evaluated for depression at this stage if the problem is not situational.

Intense disempowerment

An intense degree of disempowerment can result from chronic illness, bouts with depression or a serious social or cultural issue that knocks your entire self-concept for a loop. At this level, your loved ones may be reaching out to offer help with your clutter issue, and it may be impacting their comfort with coming to your home, especially if they have small children or mobility issues. Extreme levels of physical clutter cause so much despair that the problem is not addressed on a daily basis, or the clutter is only churned and moved about the house instead of being gradually eliminated. Intense disempowerment in the body manifests as one who ignores doctor's orders or who has multiple health issues that are not being managed effectively. Extreme insomnia, chronic fatigue, or both may be present. It is possible that disordered eating habits may have become entrenched at this stage.

Mental Clutter

Mental clutter includes all those things that fill your mind to cause stress, negative self-talk, rumination, anxiety, anger, and sadness, among other things. Mental clutter can also manifest as a full schedule, with no time for self-care. Mental clutter is deeply tied to physical clutter and spiritual clutter, as it is often the seat of issues that exacerbate both. At this point I need to make the caveat that the existence of mental clutter does not mean that mental illness does not exist. You can have both. If you have a severe mental illness, as many of us do, then no amount of mental uncluttering will cure you of the illness as well. That said, mental clutter can be stressful, and stress can trigger or exacerbate some mental illnesses. As a mentally ill person myself, the different forms of clutter directly affect how well I am able to cope. For example, if I have the physical clutter of a messy home, the physical body clutter of a lack of sleep, and the mental clutter of a busy schedule and low self-esteem, I find it completely impossible to deal with symptoms that would otherwise be easy to manage.

Are you worried that you might have a mental illness that exacerbates your clutter? This can be a concern, especially if your clutter or the mental effects of it cause your relationships to suffer, affect your ability to work or care for yourself, or cause you to be isolated in your home. Typically, seeking out therapy is the first step towards renewing your mental health. A therapist can help you get to the root of your own behaviors and help you make the right choices for your mental health. A therapist will also have a wealth of resources at his or her fingertips, which may include referrals to local physicians and professional organizers that can help you. In the back of this book is an appendix that includes a couple of resources for getting help.

Low-level maintenance needs

At this level, stressful problems continuously pop up and are prioritized before action. One's life may be full of family, friendships, obligations, work, and play in dynamic proportions that change according to the seasons and to situational factors. Emotionally, someone at this level is generally in good spirits but may have periods of self-doubt, anger, sadness, and other emotions that are appropriate to context and generally last no more than a few days at a time, with the exception of grief. Grief can affect clutter in significant ways. Not being able to let go of anything owned by a deceased loved one can be the start of a serious clutter problem. If mental illness isn't a contributing factor, attachment brought on by grief may be the problem. Self-concept is stable and high so the person seeks for internal validation more than external. A person with low-level maintenance needs may appear to others as calm, dependable, passionate about some things, and flexible.

Moderate overwhelm

At this level, stressful problems seem like fires that are put out continuously without time to rest in between them or strategize. Problems may elicit an immediate reaction without any logical sense of priority. A person with moderate overwhelm may begin to think that he or she suffers more misfortune than the average person. Self-doubt and low self-esteem may be so pervasive that the person

constantly reaches out for validation from romantic part-
ners, work, and other activities or relationships and feels
devastated any time positive validation is not immediately
forthcoming. If one thing in life is going wrong, it feels like
everything is going wrong. Chronic stress begins to manifest
negatively in life in many ways. A person who has moderate overwhelm may be perceived by others to be a "Debbie
Downer," flakey, inflexible, overreacting, and anxious.

Intense disempowerment

For an intensely disempowered person, as problems
arise they cannot be dealt with effectively at all. Such
problems must be ignored, or reframed or delegated to
others. At this level, a person may feel completely unable
to take on new tasks or give up old tasks. Self-esteem may
be low, and the person may constantly mentally ruminate
on mistakes or misfortunes. The friends and family of the
intensely disempowered person may be affected greatly,
or they may begin avoiding the person having this issue.
Productivity at work drops or becomes nonexistent and
physical clutter may be deeply tied to the mental clutter
at this stage of disempowerment. Somebody at this stage
may be perceived by others as depressed, a loner, sick,
unreliable, and tuned-out.

Spiritual Clutter

Spirituality is comprised of the incorporeal but vital components of the human experience. Spiritual clutter can

look very different for different people, and it's harder to put a finger on the problem as hunger for spirituality can vary across peoples' lifetimes. Spirituality does not have to mean religion but it can include your religious faith tradition if you have one. Spirituality also must include other intangibles that may be vital in your life. For me, these include values such as love, compassion, beauty, honor, justice, power, strength, grace, kindness, and sweetness. Your deepest spiritual values may be different, and that's okay. One important aspect of spirituality is faith, in a general sense. Faith does not have to mean belief in God or organized religion. Every healthy human must have faith. They may have faith that only science can explain the universe, or have faith in a higher power or just faith that the sun will rise tomorrow. The older version of the word *believe* meant "to hold dear." So I won't be asking you to follow anything blindly, but rather, to find something you can hold dear.

Low-level maintenance needs

Spirituality may take a back burner when things go awry, and that's okay. A person with low-level maintenance needs isn't necessarily satisfied with his or her spiritual life. It is okay if there's a hunger and a yearning there. A person with needs maintained at a low level does not need to be religious nor have religion "figured out." However, this person can go within to find a source of peace, and has a ritual or rhythm to which he or she can reach as a touchstone

when feeling off-balance. A person with low-level maintenance needs has faith in something and hope for the future.
Others may perceive him or her as peaceful, easy to open
up to, and a calming presence to be around, even if their
life does not seem well put together or deserving of praise.

Moderate overwhelm

A person with moderate spiritual overwhelm may be
a spiritually hungry person with no time or resources to
pursue spirituality. Conversely, this person may not be spiritually hungry at all, but who may feel pressured to follow
a religion that doesn't feel right to him or her. In either
case, moderate overwhelm feels like a life that may be filled
with the drudgery of chores and paying bills with little real
purpose or direction. A person with moderate overwhelm
searches for meaning in life with a sense of confusion. He
or she might suspect a run of bad luck in one or more
areas of life or even a curse. A person with moderate overwhelm may want to have a spiritual teacher or fellowship,
but have difficulty finding the right people to do the job.
Somebody with moderate spiritual overwhelm may seem
to others to be plagued by random misfortune. He may
seem needy or alienated.

Intense disempowerment

For religious folks, intense disempowerment feels like
a distrust of the divine and anger or sadness at what the
universal order seems to have dealt to his or her life. For
a nonreligious person, intense disempowerment feels like

a complete lack of meaning to life's actions and trajectory. At this stage, confusion may affect one's adherence to morals and ethics, as the existential crisis the person is experiencing takes away the point of "good" or "appropriate" behavior. Love might seem impossible at this stage, and the lack of connection to others may make that poor soul feel even more like a monster. A person at this stage may seem myopic, with a lack of empathy and compassion. Others may accuse people at this stage of being cruel, self-centered, or lost.

Order of Operations

Remember, the three different types of clutter can be interrelated. However, you might be at different stages of each type of clutter. For example, when I had my first child, I was physically and mentally in moderate overwhelm, but spiritually I was at a happy maintenance level. Earlier, when my husband and I first moved in together, I was physically moderately overwhelmed bordering on intense disempowerment, mentally intensely disempowered, but spiritually I was only moderately overwhelmed. What can one do to remedy the situation? When we joined households, one option was to pour all my energy into the mental clutter until it regained maintenance level, ignoring the other two. That is, in fact, what I did, but it was not necessarily the best course of action. Since the different types of clutter are in balance, it is best to try to work every type of clutter. In my case that would have meant bringing the physical and mental to the realm of moderate overwhelm, then gradually lowering all three types of clutter simultaneously to maintenance level.

Why work on the types of clutter simultaneously? This may seem like a foolish endeavor for an overwhelmed person, but it is the only way this works. Otherwise, you will always be juggling and playing catch up with one or the other neglected realms of your life instead of reaching your goals of clearing clutter. Consider the financial planner's classic advice for keeping financial balance. Imagine your finances as a three-legged table. One leg is your savings account, another is your debt, and the third leg is your normal everyday expenditures. When somebody is in severe debt, the immediate reaction is to quit saving money and spend every extra penny on paying off debts. It might feel very difficult or even silly to save your pennies when your wages are being garnished. However, what happens to the person when an emergency hits and there is no savings money to buffer the issue? A three-legged table cannot stand. The wise financial advisor advises placing money in all three of these priorities as needed to maintain balance. It is the same for your own physical, mental, and spiritual clutter clearing practices.

There are some exceptions to the rule of maintaining balance, and to explain why, I'd like to introduce Maslow's hierarchy of needs. Abraham Maslow was a psychologist who proposed a theory that humans need to take care of the physical (physiological, security, and safety) before the

mental (love, belonging, self-esteem), and the mental before the spiritual (self-actualization). Obviously, somebody
starving in a war-torn country will not be going on blind
dates to find love or touring new churches to find religious fellowship before finding food to eat and safe shelter. If you are suffering from physiological clutter, such as
hoarding to the extent that it threatens your health, you'll
need to tackle that before dealing with mental and spiritual clutter. If you're suffering from severe mental illness,
you'll need to work first on stabilizing and managing your
mental health before you are in the right frame of mind to
seriously consider your spiritual needs. This is why I've or-
dered the clutter types by priority in this book. However,
if you are physically and mentally safe and healthy, I urge
you to step outside of your comfort zone and embrace all
three types of clearing clutter simultaneously.

Clearing Clutter: Three Steps

Throughout this book, you'll be using three simple steps
to clear clutter. If three steps sounds too easy, just remember that you'll also be doing the balancing act between the
three types of clutter, which is a significant enough challenge to warrant simple steps. Admittedly, clearing clutter
is easier said than done. I'll introduce the three steps now,
and you'll get to see lots of applications and concrete examples in the upcoming chapters.

Simplify, harmonize, and reflect

The three steps to clearing clutter are first to simplify, then to harmonize, and finally to reflect. Think of these as a cycle, which will repeat. I'll go over each step in turn. Remember that this cycle can be used for any type of clutter. I've made the steps of the cycle universal so they can offer a philosophy and lifestyle change anyone can embrace. One of the roughest things about clearing clutter is that it is a cycle that must be maintained. You can't just finish it, place your hands on your hips and declare the job done forever. So, the process has to be a pleasant one. If you're an impulsive, action-oriented person like I am, dive into the first step with enthusiasm and optimism. If you're the sort of person who likes to plan before taking action, pour yourself a cup of tea or sit down to meditate as you go through the steps. Just don't forget to actually take the next step.

Step 1: Simplify

Think of the simplest lifestyle that you can achieve. One that will give you space and time to pursue your dreams, stretch yourself, and grow to your full potential. Hold that vision. Imagine that it is already in place and think about what you will be able to do with your new freedom. Now, you must achieve this by simplifying. You may need to begin by stopping or managing the inflow of new clutter. Then, decide where the existing clutter and future clutter will go to move through your life without interrupting your energy flow. Depending on the type of clutter, this may mean tapping into your generosity, your boundary-setting skills and your resourcefulness. Simplification is a pruning stage, clearing away old negativity, habits that no longer serve you, and things or connections that have outlived their usefulness. Get rid of anything that doesn't give you joy or doesn't fit into your values. Be merciless.

Step 2: Harmonize

This is a maintenance stage, where you work to get used to the new normal. If you've put off any decisions when simplifying, at this stage you can give your simplified life a trial run to make sure it works for you. If there are any kinks in your productivity or energy flow, at this stage you can work to smooth them out or make some gentle shifts in your lifestyle to accommodate them as needed. To harmonize, it is vital to check in with all three realms of life, the physical, mental, and spiritual, to nurture any areas that may have been lacking. Once you simplify one area of life, those raw edges of new growth elsewhere or areas of your life with severe lack may become more apparent to you. At this stage, be gentle with yourself, and allow yourself the time to make mistakes and play catch-up while you learn to maintain the new normal without sliding back into old habits. The first time you go through the "simplify, harmonize, and reflect" cycle, this phase may be a doozy. However, once you get used to the clearing clutter way of life, this phase will act more as a quick touchstone to balance out your physical, mental, and spiritual self.

Step 3: Reflect

Only after you feel like you've gotten into your groove with the changes you've made should you reflect upon the process that you've undertaken. What does your immediate intuition tell you about the changes you've made? What went well about the process? What went poorly? Now is the time to take a hard look at your behaviors, as you gear up for another cycle of Simplifying. At this stage, revisit your goals and decide whether your expectations are still clear and reasonable. Will you keep wearing down the mountain if you cycle through the steps again? As long as there is progress, however slow or small, you are succeeding and can continue to move forward and tweak your process as needed during the first two steps. Give yourself a reward. If you've stalled out, it may be because you need to change the simplification process or to work harder on balancing all areas of your life during the harmonizing phase. Remember, no person has had to deal with clutter only once in life, so everyone is going to have to repeat the cycle. There's no shame in it.

Find Your True Valuables

One of the most difficult parts of this process is simplification. Unlike the harmonizing phase, which gets easier as you learn to be mindful of areas of your life that may have been previously neglected, it is always hard to let go during the simplification step. One way to be consistent and less arbitrary during simplification is to prune your life down to your core values. If the physical, mental, or spiritual clutter isn't aligned with your values, it's time to get rid of it. Simple as that. It's time to do a journal activity that will help you with the process, no matter what domain of life you're examining.

Start by brainstorming life values. What is truly valuable to you? For example, "health" is one common valuable thing in peoples' lives, perhaps "family" is another for you. Circle each of your values and draw lines to connect any that may be related to one another. This style of brainstorming will help you expand your thoughts while categorizing them. If you struggle with this, try thinking about what you spend money on and what values you're trying to reach with that expenditure.

Next, get to the core of each value so it makes sense in any context and reflects the truth of who you are. Try to translate some tangible values to the intangible. For example, even if you value your television-watching time, cross out "TV" and write down "recreation" if what you really value is that downtime. If you wrote down something general like "money," find out whether your root value is actually "stability," "freedom," or something else. I wrote down "travel," which I could distill down to a love of "learning" and "adventure," but I can still keep all three words on the page if they still make sense in my physical, mental, and spiritual clutter-clearing context, so I drew a line from the "travel" bubble connected to two other bubbles representing those other values.

Clean up your list of true valuables to a shorter list of the most important. Order these numerically from the most important value to least. When you feel stuck in the simplification process for any area of your life, look back to this journal page. If what you're keeping in your life doesn't fit into any of your root values, prune it out of your life. Learn the values by heart; that way, the list itself won't turn into yet another piece of clutter.

Baby Steps

Being gentle with yourself means taking small steps, but it also means no stalling. Think: Relentless forward motion. I'm an impulsive person, so this is easy for me, but I recognize that it can be challenging for others. One thing that helps me is taking a small step toward my goal right away, even if it's late at night and you've just finished reading this first chapter. Small steps might be researching some information about your goal, setting an appointment on your calendar (yes, even if it's with yourself to get to work on something personal), or moving some money into your savings account for a project. Taking that first baby step helps other steps follow. The more steps you take, the less time you spend in between taking them, and the path will seem easier as you go. It will soon feel less like pulling teeth and more like following your bliss.

"Realize what the essentials of life are—such as warmth when you are cold, a dry spot on a rainy day, the simplest food when you are hungry, pure cool water when you are thirsty. You soon put material things in their proper place, realizing that they are there for use, but relinquishing them when they are not useful. You soon experience and learn to appreciate the great freedom of simplicity."

....

Peace Pilgrim

Two

·············

Physical Clutter:
Home, Office, Car, and Body

When my husband and I first moved in together, our physical clutter merged to create a mess of epic proportions. We had barely any real furniture. In fact, I can list all of our furniture right here: Futon, two shoddy computer desks, two barstools at the kitchen counter, and a TV table that had been crafted from spare lumber with ugly carelessness. The clutter was horrific. Less furniture does not necessarily mean less clutter. In fact, it can mean vastly more clutter as there are no drawers, stand-alone cabinets, entertainment centers, dressers, or bureaus in which clutter can hide. The main storage closet was filled with empty boxes from floor to ceiling. In general, the living space felt cramped, dark, and impossible to keep clean. It took my family about three days of cleaning to reduce the clutter, but that wasn't all.

My poor car was so cluttered that an actual pack rat had made a nest of string and candy wrappers deep in the well of the spare tire.

....

Clearing-Clutter Tip: Before you get started, it may help you to perform a quick ritual exercise to get yourself in the right headspace.

Untie any laces or strings on the clothing you are wearing to loosen the way.

Rub your hands together briskly and feel the tingle as you pull them apart from one another slowly. Some people believe this tingle is the spiritual energy of your body, but it is actually the blood flowing in the veins at the surface of your hands.

Clap three times loudly or ring a bell. Many cultures clap or ring bells to frighten away pixies or spirits that might cause clutter as mischief, or to shake free and loosen stuck energy in the clutter.

Get a glass of water to hydrate yourself and put in a squeeze of lemon for energy and clarity. Pause before you get started and visualize your clutter already cleared.

Chant: "Source of flame, earth, wind, and water. Within and without, clearing clutter." Take a sip of the water, set down your glass and begin. You can tie your shoelaces again if necessary!

....

Simplify, Harmonize, and Reflect in Physical Space

The home is often where the worst clutter piles. It's our nesting space. The crossroads where we find rest and relief and through which all of our belongings pass. We prepare food there, we sleep there, and we invite others into our homes. For some, the clutter reaches hoarding levels, and begins to threaten our feeling of security and even safety, thus precluding any hope of developing self-esteem, a sense of love and belonging, or spiritual self-actualization. Thus, many of the tips in this chapter will be written for the context of a living space, but could also be applied to a car or work space. More specific tips to shared spaces like an office will be included in chapter 5, since the office is not necessarily yours to shape as you will.

Simplify your physical space

Healthy and balanced people go through regular cycles of pruning down as many things as they acquire in order to keep circulating possessions like energy throughout their lives. If you're new to this process, you may have to do a big purge or many small ones right away. Read all of the simplification instructions before you get started. Upon evaluating your own personal situation, you may decide that you need extra resources, like some helping hands or a rented trash dumpster, before you begin. If you share your living space with other people, enlist in their help or at least warn them before you get to work. Some people, especially my husband in particular, find it disorienting and stressful to have their personal clutter items moved by somebody else.

You'll need some bags or boxes to start. Have one each for garbage and recycling, and have another for giving away to a local charity that has a drop-off point for belongings. Throwing away things might feel difficult for you. I have trouble even throwing away broken or expired things sometimes. Inoculate yourself against those feelings by practicing the necessary evil of ridding your life of waste. Don't beat yourself up about it. I like to take the opportunity to transform those feelings into a renewed commitment to curb my acquisition of things that might be a burden on our environment when they eventually must be discarded.

As a kid, I didn't pick up after myself, but my preschool teacher knew that I cared about the environment, so she equated the toys and things in the classroom to litter. Since I detested litter, when she related the toys to litter, I understood and learned my lesson. Garbage is garbage whether it is in a landfill or in your home wasting space. Everything you own will be discarded eventually, whether it is now or in a hundred years. Take a deep breath and start throwing things away and gathering things to donate. Hold in your mind the vision of what you want your life and environment to look like after you're finished.

....

Clearing-Clutter Tip: Avoid churning, where your possessions simply move from place to place in your home while you decide what to do with them.

Maybe you move all your clothes from the floor to the bed before sorting them, or you move some things to the hallway while you decide whether to give them away or not.

When you're clearing clutter, pick an item up and pretend that it is stuck to your hand until you make a final decision whether to keep it, discard it, or give it away.

....

Don't get carried away with saving things for others, as this is one point that can trip up many cluttered lives. If your physical clutter problem is moderate to severe, don't set aside lots of things for sale unless you need the money to survive. Reselling used stuff is a full-time job in and of itself. At home, I have one cupboard reserved for things I need to return, things to give to a specific person, and new gifts for re-gifting. I make sure to cycle through all of those as quickly as possible so the cupboard is more empty than full. Don't get caught in the trap of saving lots of stuff with the rationale that somebody you know is bound to use it. Tap into your compassionate side and donate it. Don't deprive yourself of useful storage space and imagine that you'll free it up by foisting things on an unsuspecting friend or relative. They don't actually need all that stuff.

Now comes the tough part: deciding what to keep. Try to keep only those things that bring you joy every time you look at them. Use this philosophy as a touchstone. Recall your list of what things are most valuable to you. Sure, a toothbrush might not bring you joy when you look at it, but if heath is at the top of your list, it will bring you joy overall. And if a prettier or more effective toothbrush would bring you greater joy, by all means discard the old one and make room for the new.

Decide how much time you want to spend before you take a break. This will depend on your personality. For me, my house is now generally uncluttered, so I have to zero in on the small vortices where clutter gathers such as where new mail or belongings get deposited, the dreaded cluttered coffee table where I study, my bedside table piles of books, and the bathroom cupboards where unused products seem to gather like mice. I like to work on the small disaster areas for fifteen minutes at a time, but some people do best with larger chunks of time like a couple of hours or even a full day for a big clutter clearing job. When you stop, make sure you put your next clearing clutter date on your calendar if you need the reminder or motivation.

....

Clearing-Clutter Tip: Make yourself a "maybe" box if you're ever *really* torn about whether or not to keep something. This way, you'll have a box to put into storage with a date on it that marks when you need to use it or lose it.

For example, I often get myself into art projects or musical instruments I don't have time to practice.

I put some craft supplies and other things into a box and set a deadline so that it would either get used or get out of my house. I put the box in my garage. When I hadn't opened it by its deadline, I had nearly forgotten what was inside. I took the entire box to donate without opening it.

Don't use a "maybe" box if you've got a serious clutter problem to the point of hoarding, because your whole place is already your "maybe" box!

....

Get rid of all of the bulky things that tend to creep in on your living space. I'm sure you know the sorts of things I'm talking about. The objects that you moved into the hallway "just for a minute" or onto the kitchen counter "for now" and just left there for months or even years on end. Those things become part of your landscape and blend into your life so much that you might even step over some of these objects every day, ignored until the day you will supposedly give it away or fix it or install it or do whatever it was you meant to do in the first place. Subconsciously, those things affect you, but it only comes up to your conscious mind when guests come to your home and wonder why that thing is dominating the room. Try looking at your living space with the eyes of someone visiting for the first time. People who live in cluttered homes often become "clutter-blind," meaning that what may seem like oppressive and shocking clutter to outsiders seems normal to them. Even the spouses and children of such people may become habituated and clutter-blind to chaos and disorder that may have seemed upsetting and abnormal at one time. If you suspect that you are clutter-blind, get some outside perspective in the simplification process.

Before you put things away, clean everything. Wipe down shelves and dust things you put away. Be mindful of where you place things and leave enough space for regular cleaning, and arrange your things so they are pleasing to the eye. You may need to pull everything away from the area you're clearing or even empty a room into a hallway before putting everything back. Now is the time to get out the vacuum cleaner and the broom. Your lungs will thank you after you clear out all that dust and detritus. Don't forget to clear closets, drawers, and other hidden spaces. Even if your own eyes or the eyes of your guests don't see the clutter, it still affects your energy. For example, I tend to collect papers and files long after they're no longer needed. I once found bank statements that were decades old. Whenever I need to find an important document, it's stressful to have to first thumb through excessive worthless documents to find it, even if things are logically organized. I have to force myself to destroy old documents regularly to keep the clutter at bay for those important moments when I need to find something.

My kitchen clutter days ended when I followed the advice of my best friend and started storing away countertop appliances between uses. My kitchen was tiny, so I procured a small plastic rack for this job. Later, I moved to a place with a pantry that could accommodate my appliances. Without mixers, food processors, blenders, toasters, rice cookers, and more cluttering up the countertop, I could easily wipe counters clean. The small hassle of getting them out and putting them away afterwards was totally worth it for the wide expanse of workspace that opened up. As a bonus, I always remember to clean the appliances before putting them away, so they don't become more dingy and gross.

....

Clearing–Clutter Tip: In Jewish tradition, the family dining room table is like an altar or sacred space. I believe that this tradition should be practiced in every home.

Don't let your dining room table be a place of clutter. Keep it clear; engage in the ritual of place setting.

While at the table, don't tolerate any bad manners from your children or yourself, and put away all distractions to engage in the moment with your food and pleasant company.

Don't place objects on your dining room table that don't belong there, like mail, clothes, or shoes in between meals.

....

When you finally finish your simplification process, at least for one round, move the bags out of your house as quickly as possible. Walk the trash bags out to the trash, or make the car trip to the dump and donation drop-off. Don't allow yourself any time to agonize over the chore, because you need to move onto the next phase of harmonizing. The simplification isn't done until you take the last chore of removing the clutter from your home off your "to do" list. Once the items are gone, you won't be able to second-guess yourself, and that's a good thing. Worrying about the feelings you'll have is much worse than actually experiencing the feelings that come when you rid yourself of your clutter. In fact, those feelings may be more life-affirming than grieving.

Harmonize your physical space

After completing a simplification cycle, you'll go through an adjustment period. It may be particularly intense if you just did your first major clutter clearing session in your living space. Now you're harmonizing, getting used to the new normal, which is key for balancing out your life. During this phase, start by thinking about what you may have been neglecting in your emotional and intellectual lives as well as your spiritual life. Now you will pay attention to and nurture these areas, which may seem counterintuitive when you're already reeling after a major lifestyle overhaul in simplifying your surroundings. It is important, however, to fill the void you've left with spirituality and

brain food rather than leaving it open and gaping or allowing it to refill with possessions.

Stemming the tide of new items can feel problematic
for somebody whose life is imbalanced. You might feel
unable to pass up a good deal. You might buy multiples of
things you already have because of a bargain or because
you like the security of knowing you'll always have more
of your favorite shampoo or brand of food. Just keep in
mind that you don't live in a culture of lack. It is okay to
trust that the universe will provide for you through the
proper channels as it has all your adult life. Passing up on
a good deal is worth it if it helps you battle your own
clutter demons. Or, as my dad always used to say, "If the
pleasure of not doing it outweighs the pleasure of doing it,
let it go." Developing a source of trust and faith that you
will always be resourceful enough to have plenty may be
spiritual work you need to do.

Stick to a list when you go shopping. Don't go grocery shopping while hungry and, for the same reason,
don't go clothes shopping when you're dressed in your
pajamas and feeling unhappy about your looks. When you
go to get groceries, keep to the outside edges of the store
where the essentials like produce are kept, and venture
into the inner aisles only for specific necessary items on
your shopping list. If you do see something you want that
you weren't expecting to buy, consider sleeping on that
decision. Ask yourself if you have an immediate use for
that item today or on a specific date you can name in the

future, and if your house has a permanent place for that item to live. If neither of those are true, pass on buying the item to stick to your goal of being clutter free.

Avoid using "retail therapy" to treat emotional ills. Find a more healthy reward, release from boredom, or source of comfort for yourself. If you find yourself turning to retail therapy, that's a sign that your emotional clutter needs to be cleared. My own weakness is the "bargain" lure of garage sales and thrift shops. I make sure I only bring home things that will bring me joy and that will have a proper place in my life, which also means balancing my treasure hunting with clearing clutter.

....

Clearing-Clutter Tip: Reframing the gift-giving holidays and occasions may be part of balancing your new life and your life goals.

Encourage your friends and family to give you experiences instead of stuff. A zoo membership or tickets to a concert may be a much better gift for you than yet another possession.

Strive to give the same sorts of gifts to others. Not only will it clue them in that you are serious, but you will also get to bypass the problem of storing gifts for others in your house until you're able to give them away.

When you receive gifts, don't automatically unseal the packaging and think about where you'll put them. Decide first whether to return, regift, donate, or keep.

....

Maintaining a cleaning regimen for your newly simplified space will be a big part of getting to know your new life, and it will serve as a trial for keeping things simple. There is thought to be a universal magical law that "like attracts like." That is, a cluttered home will seem to accumulate even more clutter. An unclean home will encourage occupants to live in a cluttered space. When clearing clutter from your home, cleaning has to be a necessary harmonizing component after you've simplified the amount of stuff and space you have to clean.

If you're new to starting a cleaning habit, it may feel particularly daunting. I know, because cleaning my house is pretty new to me as an adult. As a child, I was blessed with a mother who spoiled me and cleaned up after me wherever I went. As a result, I had a pretty steep learning curve when I finally needed to grow up—and I'm still in the process. What worked for me was setting aside specific days of the week for specific rooms. After the process of clearing clutter was through, I started with a pretty rigid plan: Monday was cleaning the kitchen and dining room, Tuesday was the two bathrooms and the hallway (as well as the baseboards), Wednesday was the living room and washing windows, Thursday was the bedroom and laundry, including bed sheets, Friday was mopping the whole house and working on the yard. Every day involved sweeping the floor and vacuuming furniture since I have indoor pets. I tried to give myself weekends off. Now that I have a clutter-free home and am into the groove of keeping it that way, I don't have such a rigid schedule. But for any new lifestyle change, some guidelines are helpful.

Tackling your home's dishes and the laundry monster may be quite the battle. First, you'll need to give yourself a system, and this may be different for every family. Do you need laundry baskets in every bedroom? Can the family use a laundry room as a central zone for collecting such stuff? Try running a load of laundry every day. For me, this works best if I start a load right after I put my kids to bed. That way, I run it all the way through the wash and dry cycle before my own bedtime. Doing laundry every day might sound like a hassle, but it is far less of a hassle than dealing with a mountain of laundry intermittently and having the task chatter in the back of your mind more than once a day. If you build a load of laundry into your routine, you'll barely notice the impact on your life except the positive outcome. Try this method for a few months, long enough to make it a habit. Then, reevaluate how many clothes you need if you're doing laundry more often. Your clothes may need to run through a simplification process now.

For those of you who loathe doing dishes so much that you've resorted to using paper plates, you may find that you use fewer dishes when you start building it into your schedule. I like to do the dishes right before bed. Now that I have a dishwasher, the task is pretty simple, someone loads the dishwasher throughout the day, finishes right before bed, and pushes the button. In the morning, I unload the dishwasher and put everything away. If you make sure to scrub your sink every day, this task can be a tool to help you do the rest of your daily duties. After all, you can't scrub your sink until it is free of dishes, and this can help spur you to begin the process of collecting dishes throughout the house and making sure they're all washed and ready for the day to come. Later in this chapter, you can read about a similar practice of washing your floors to represent a symbolic cleansing, plus an aid to motivate you to get the floors clean enough for a floor wash.

....

Clearing-Clutter Tip: The broom is more than just a cleaning tool. It is a symbol for clearing clutter and inviting abundance and fertility blessings into your home.

Sweep often, and make sweeping a special ritual that readies you for guests, special time with family, or simply sweeping away thoughts of a stressful work day.

Visualize negativity being swept away. Choose an attractive broom and store it standing with the bristles up for good luck and to preserve the bristles.

Folklore says that when your broom falls over, it means company is coming. You can bless your broom or even a vacuum by sprinkling it with salt water and passing it through frankincense incense.

You can write on the broom stick, with the words traveling toward the bristles, "I sweep in clarity, simplicity, and peace." On the other side, with the words traveling away from the bristles write, "I sweep out clutter."

A new home should always mean buying a new broom. Leave old brooms and dishrags in the house or apartment when you sell it or move away. You don't want to bring dirt and grime from the past into your new life.

....

An important part of the harmonizing step will be inviting people over to your home regularly. I advise this for several reasons. First of all, you're tending to your emotional and intellectual needs for good conversation. This will help you to balance out the clearing of clutter from your mind, body, and spirit. Having company coming can also be an incentive to clean and clear some last-minute stubborn clutter like unopened mail or bathroom dust bunnies. And when other people come into your space, having that outsider perspective can assist in ensuring you aren't simply habituated to your clutter. When I was getting ready to have a baby, a young child who was a guest in my home advised me that my bathroom would have to be "much cleaner" when the baby arrived. I appreciated her honesty. Likewise, my dad was always a great, honest critic of my housekeeping. Don't shy away from people who are blunt about your housekeeping habits. Your habit may be to take these comments personally, but instead use them as resources to help your self-improvement.

Your physical space: Reflection

How did it go? What did you notice about the process of simplifying and harmonizing your life? What was surprisingly easy and what was too hard? Have you noticed other people saying things about your process? Were they compliments or criticisms? Take some time to note your energy level after doing all this work. If you overdid things, you might want to shoot for less effort next time around. If you still feel energized, perhaps you can step things up a notch. Is your cleaning routine working out for you now that you've cleared some of the clutter? There are a number of barriers you might have to smash through before you do another even more successful round of simplifying your life.

······································

Clearing-Clutter Tip: Are you a visual person? Go easy on yourself. Some people just can't deal with having all their belongings tucked away neatly in drawers.

My husband is visual and would rather have his clean clothes in a pile on the floor where he can see them than have them folded and stacked in a drawer. We compromised with cubbies and hanging clothes so he can see what he wants to wear while still being organized. Many of his other belongings collect neatly in baskets, on the bathroom counter, on the bedroom credenza, and near where he keeps his laptop. This way he can see his things close at hand, but I can still keep them contained and easily pick up the baskets to clean surfaces underneath.

······································

Take note if you find evidence that you've been thinking about things the wrong way, also called "cognitive distortion." It's a natural human reaction to avoid the anxiety associated with a loss of possessions or anything else
for that matter. For example, if your loved ones have been
telling you you're hanging onto garbage or that you're
never going to get around to fixing those old clothes or
pieces of furniture but you're *certain* that's not the case,
you might be experiencing a cognitive distortion. If you'd
like to believe that you can get rid of or deal with those
things and clear your clutter, try replacing the old scripts
playing over and over again in your head with new ones.
You may find yourself thinking, "I just need time—when
I'm not feeling stressed—to fix these broken things." Try
to replace that thought with, "I can throw away this old
broken thing and get a better version later if I feel like it."
Instead of thinking, "Grandma gave me this before she
died and I am scared to let go of the memory of her,"
think, "My memory of Grandma lives forever in my heart.
I can throw this away without it affecting my relationship
with her or how she's affected my life."

Did any feelings arise when you were getting rid of
things or trying to get rid of things? Many people experience at least a little anxiety when throwing something
away that might be useful or valuable. This anxiety can in-
tensify if the item has sentimental value as well. The only
way to cure yourself of this anxiety is to practice gradual
exposure to that feeling, because you may be holding onto

clutter to avoid this confrontation. When you pick up an object in your home and sense that you may be choosing to keep it "for no good reason," stop and rate your anxiety on a scale of one to ten. Pretend that an anxiety rating of one means that it's no big deal to get rid of the thing and an anxiety rating of ten means that you would regret it for the rest of your life and grieve as though a loved one had died if you were to part with the thing. If your rating is a five or above, don't get rid of it yet, even if you know in your heart it is just garbage—you're just not ready.

Walk around your house rating things until you find one that has a lower anxiety rating, like a three. Think about what is making you feel anxious about giving it away and put those thoughts into sentences. Sometimes it helps when the sentences sound silly when spoken aloud, like, "I'm afraid that if I get rid of this extra coat I will not be able to afford a new coat in the future when the one I use now wears out because I might simultaneously lose my job on a cold winter's day." Once you've given voice to all your fears, face them and throw the item away. Make sure the item is out of your possession that same day, preferably within the hour. Walk the trash to the curb or drop off the donation at your charity of choice.

Next, sit for a moment and own any anxiety you feel over getting rid of the thing. Don't distract yourself from the feeling, and don't judge yourself. Just let the emotion wash over you and reflect on it. Is your anxiety rating accurate? Do you feel more or less anxious than you expected?

Wait until the next day and then rate your feelings again. Has your anxiety subsided? If you feel ready, pick an item that has a higher anxiety level rating and try again.

During your reflection process, avoid letting an all-or-nothing attitude keep you from starting the "simplify, harmonize, and reflect" cycle all over again. I tend to fall into that trap when cleaning house; if I can't keep my house looking the way I want it to look, then what's the point of, say, washing windows, period? They'll just get dirty again, after all. This is when I know that I'm cluttering up my spiritual life with concerns that are distracting me from being joyful, and I need to seek balance. Instead of becoming too attached to the outcome of a house that conforms exactly to my vision, I try to focus on finding a little joy in the process. I put on some music and sing or chant while remaining mindful that I'm doing the work for my family and for myself. You can learn more about spiritual principles that can help balance out your "all or nothing" focus in chapter 4.

Finally, don't forget to celebrate your achievement and your efforts as you close your reflection phase. You've put in a lot of work. Even if you didn't quite reach the goal you envisioned, you still made a lot more progress toward that goal than you would have sitting around ignoring your clutter. Think of some ways you can reward yourself that won't add to your clutter; indulge in a little pampering before you start the cycle anew.

....

Clearing-Clutter Tip: Sometimes, you have to work on mental or spiritual clutter before you can really tackle your physical clutter. This can be frustrating because a home in chaos may not be encouraging for mental and spiritual healing. If this is the case for you, find a place outside the home that is clear of clutter and where you can find calm.

It's all the better if your calm place is in nature like a garden, country field, or a wooded path. Richard Louv, author of *The Nature Principle*, speculated that people can suffer from "nature deficit disorder," and that reconnection to nature can be a key part of being emotionally and physically healthy.

....

Cleaning: Spiritual Floor Washes

When developing a cleaning regimen, it can be helpful to create barriers against the clutter that hinders further cleaning. The example I gave earlier is to make sure to scrub your sink every night, a practice that entails washing any dishes in the sink and thus inhibiting dish clutter. Another way to do this is by regularly mopping or vacuuming your floors. I am already motivated enough to clean my kitchen, but I struggle with finding inspiration to clean my floors frequently enough for a growing family with pets. It helps to assign yourself a day of the week to use your floor wash to mop all the hard floors in your home. This will encourage you to clear the clutter so that the task can be done with regularity.

Spiritual floor washes can be a way to positively influence the energy in your household and cultivate a practice of cleansing for your family to clear clutter away. The practice of spiritual floor washing comes from Latin American and American Hoodoo traditions. In the culture of such families, the smell of the herbal floor wash and the sound of the head of the household singing while mopping the floors is a comforting part of regular family life and a memory children bring to their adult lives and habits.

Traditionally, floor washes are made by boiling herbs in water and adding just a bit of salt—not enough to scour the hardwood or tile but enough for salt to be a symbol of cleanliness. Nothing harmful can grow in an environment too salty, after all, and in witchcraft salt is considered to be earth of the earth. The herbs used in the floor washes vary widely, and each family may develop their own favorite. Floor washes are sold in some stores, and you can also make them with your favorite herbs. Choose herbs with a scent you enjoy. Use a floor wash as a mop solution or put it in a spray bottle to spritz on your carpet before vacuuming. Another alternative for rugs or carpets is to sprinkle a dry herb like lavender and a pinch of salt before vacuuming or beating the rug outside.

A purification floor wash could be a strained tea of bay leaves, marjoram, and rosemary. You can also wash windows and doors with this tea. Lemon juice squeezed into water can clear a home of negativity and energetic clutter. For a clearing clutter floor wash designed for blessing you with clarity of mind, try using white vinegar and lemon peels. Drop a small piece of fluorite or other crystal into the bucket or spray bottle. If you don't have fluorite, you can use a rock you find outside that has a vein of quartz.

For a floor wash that invites harmony into your home, try using essential oils of tangerine and grapefruit and a teaspoon of sea salt. If you don't have the essential oils, you can soak grapefruit peels and juicy tangerine pits in the vinegar and then strain out the detritus before using it. An alternate harmony recipe is to use some lavender and rose. After a heated argument that disrupts the harmony, you can try a more serious mixture of peppermint, lavender, spearmint, and rose. If the disharmony is caused by some upset outside the home, make a tea of parsley as a floor wash. If the disharmony began within the home, make a tea with valerian root as a floor wash. Be careful though, valerian is a powerful herb that has a strong odor. I mix a tiny bit of it with chamomile to mask the smell, but if you don't like it you can stick with the grapefruit and tangerine harmony floor wash.

For a happy home, create a floor wash with vanilla and tangerine. For a floor wash that invites helpful house spirits and fairies that tidy up while you sleep, mix some lavender, spearmint and vanilla in your floor wash. To clear your mind and reduce stress, try a floor wash with lavender and peppermint.

As you can see, with just a few herbs on hand, you can mix up floor washes for a variety of uses. When I make a spiritual floor wash, I make a four thieves vinegar. Legend has it that, when the plague swept across Europe, four mysterious thieves would rob the dead by anointing themselves with a healing, protecting, and cleansing potion. Many recipes abound. I like to use three pints white vinegar mixed with four herbs, one for each of the thieves. Herbs that were traditionally used have clearing properties: Lavender, mint, rosemary, garlic, thyme, and sage. Again, pick ones you like (or the ones you already have on hand) and add three pinches of salt. I heat up the vinegar and steep the herbs in the solution. Then, I strain the liquid into spray bottles I use to clean surfaces. I cut the vinegar with water to create a floor wash.

....

Clearing-Clutter Tip: Have you experienced a lot of accidents around your kitchen? It may be time to spiritually cleanse the area. Here are some tips based on research by Scott Cunningham and David Harrington in *The Magical Household*.

Boil water in a copper tea kettle and add three bay leaves, rosemary, lemon peel, and cinnamon.

Scatter a pinch of salt on your floor, sweep it all up, and get rid of it outside your home. Strain the water in the tea kettle.

Tie two old dishrags together and soak them in the water. Use the water as a floor wash and for cleaning surfaces and appliances in your kitchen.

Pour the leftover water outside on the earth and bury the knotted rags.

··································

A variation of the floor wash idea can be used to clear clutter from your car and to bless it with protective energies. Start by clearing any garbage or clutter from inside your car. Remember that anything sitting freely in your car can become a projectile in an accident. A friend of my family was hit by another car while driving and he said that his daughter's Barbie dolls that cluttered the back seat became missiles. Thank goodness she wasn't in the car at the time!

After you've removed as much clutter as you can, clean the car from roof to tires with a tea made with protective herbs such as rosemary, bay leaves, or dill; whichever scent you can handle works. You can add soap to this concoction to make the car wash more than spiritual. Wipe down the dash and interior surfaces and sprinkle a bit of the tea on any carpet you can vacuum.

Spring Cleaning

There's something magical about springtime. The warmer weather in some climates may allow people to throw open the windows and let in some fresh air. The allure of springtime activities might require you to dig out lawn equipment and pack away winter clothes. Bright and cheerful people and animals with spring fever inspire action and movement. This may be why spring cleaning is so pervasive in our culture.

Even if you've never undertaken a spring cleaning, you might want to mark it on your calendar for near the spring equinox, around March 20 or 21 in the Northern Hemisphere, and in September in the Southern. The spring equinox is celebrated in some cultures as a time of rebirth and rejuvenation, good for starting over with a clean slate and watching new and pleasant things grow in your life. It is a good time to pull weeds from the garden, in some climates, to make room for newly planted seeds. In warmer regions, spring cleaning might actually begin in early February, as a representation of the first stirrings of life in deep winter. Imagine shaking the clutter free from the house after feeling like you've been buried under the winter accumulation of stuff from the holidays and the many weeks or months of indoor activities. It is good luck to wash your face on May 1 with the morning dew collected from leaves and flowers.

Whenever the sunshine and warm outdoor weather tells you it is springtime, take the opportunity to open your windows and doors and sweep all the dirt out of your home. Clear out any clutter that has accumulated over the winter months, especially any objects that haven't been used in the last six months. Donate them so that somebody else can use them. Consider bringing in some freshly cut flowers to bless your clean environment with the positive energy of spring.

....

Clearing-Clutter Tip: Some other symbolically good times to clean are when the moon is waning. This represents the fading of energies, so you can use the moon's symbolic energy to empower you.

As the moon wanes, so can your clutter also fade from your life. Saturday is a good day of the week to rid your life of clutter, as it is associated with the god Saturn (Greek: Kronos), who governs order and chaos.

Use the energy of Saturn to inspire you to throw away or get rid of anything in your life that no longer serves you.

....

Ritual for Giving Things Away

For some people, giving things away is more than just tossing garbage. Some people prefer to rehome furniture or other belongings with the same care given in adopting or rehoming a beloved pet. I've also heard stories of people who feel guilt at not being able to give better things away to charity. Personally, I've never been particularly wealthy, so giving small amounts of cash away to charitable causes made me anxious, almost as if it wasn't worth the embarrassment to offer such a small gift. I also have the dubious honor of actually having a chair be rejected by Goodwill because the fabric had been penetrated with too much pet hair to be usable for anyone else. Now, of course giving away garbage in such a state should always be avoided!

If you do have something of value you must give away, here's a ritual you can use to add value to your gift.

First, you'll need a bit of cinnamon, which is meant to magically multiply and improve your gift so that more and better gifts will soon be drawn to the chosen charity. Sprinkle the cinnamon on your giveaway items. Next, the following prayer should be spoken as close as possible as to the time you drop off the items. Just before or just after is okay if you're shy and don't want the volunteer staff to catch you murmuring over your stuff.

> Be as a seed, a seed for change.
> Allow my gift to grow and rearrange.
> Multiply blessings for many.
> For those with none, let there be plenty.

Retreat from your gift without looking back, but don't forget your receipt for tax write-off purposes. As soon as you return home, find one more item to put aside for donation as an act of following through with your prayer. You multiplying the items you prayed over will cause that energy to radiate throughout the universe and encourage others with more to do the same.

Purification

Sometimes, even after the clutter is cleared out of a place, you can have the sinking feeling that there is some sort of unseen clutter in the room. This can even happen in a garden, where garden pests might be the culprit of that sinking feeling. Ancient peoples would write stern notes to home and garden pests asking them to vacate the premises. Or they found it helpful to burn a dishrag the first time thunder was heard in March. However, for indoors a purification exercise might be more effective. Even in an empty room that has seen a lot of arguments in its day, or that was the site of a murder or suicide, some sensitive people will be able to feel energetic clutter. You might feel it as an emotion like sadness or anger. You might feel it as a general sense of unease or a creeping sensation under the skin. This could be marked by the strong but unexplained desire to leave the area. Some people will even leave a room or basement unused or move to a different apartment to avoid these sensations. Instead, you can purify to make room for good things in that space. Here is a very simple but effective purification for the beginner who can feel a bit of intangible clutter in a place.

Step 1

Visualize yourself encircled with protective energy. It might look like a purple wall of flame, a rainbow bubble, a golden sarcophagus, or even a pack of dogs. Imagine this visualization strongly and hold it in your mind's eye. If you are having trouble with this step, read more in chapter 4 about your natural protective aura.

Step 2

Sweep the space with a broom three times in a counterclockwise circle. Even if the area is carpeted or outdoors, the sweeping motion with a broom can be used to symbolically clear the air. Sweep once high in the sky, once at waist height, and once at floor level to clear the entire space.

Step 3

Speak a purification prayer. You can word your own or use something like this: "Clear the clutter of this space. Banish rubbish, harm and waste. Ward this place with protection around. Evil sink into the ground."

Step 4

Walk around the circle three times with incense; white sage is a good one to use. Add three pinches of salt to a cup of water and then circle three more times sprinkling this salted water with your fingers. Together, the salt, water and burning incense represent the four elements of earth, water, air, and fire.

Step 5

Ring a bell three times or clap your hands three times. The purification is done.

Feng Shui

Feng shui is the Chinese practice and philosophy of allowing *chi* (energy) to properly flow through a space. Recall that "energy" in the chi sense of the word represents the life force people use to manifest what they want and need. Though this energy is omnipresent, it can become diverted or stagnant. You feel this energy as soon as you pull into your driveway and the second you open your eyes in the morning. The Western interpretation of this Chinese architectural and geomantic practice brought the art to our homes and offices. It is the Western version I will use here for some practical tips.

Picture the world as a giant river and you as a salmon swimming in that river. If the river has a lot of jagged rocks, it will impede travel in that direction. Not only are those rocks obstacles for you, but they can cause the river's water flow to change. Some rocks divert the water flow, causing it to splash about chaotically. Others block the flow altogether, forming small pools that have no current where mosquitoes can breed but are of no use to you as a salmon. Feng shui is about figuratively removing these rocks from your life, moving them for optimal flow, or choosing a path unblocked by such barriers. Feng shui is a huge, very detailed discipline, so I'm going to limit it here to tips that will help you clear clutter and include some tips from Western magical traditions as well.

Generally speaking, *any* clutter is bad feng shui. The different areas of the house represent your life and can change with the orientation of your home, which is out–side the scope of this book; however, you should know that clutter can create obstacles in more than your hallway. If you've unwittingly created clutter in an area of your

home relating to love, for example, you could find yourself stuck in a romance rut. You won't notice freedom in
your love life until you clear that clutter. This may be one
reason why the act of clearing clutter can feel so good.

To help chi enter and move about your home freely,
clear clutter away from lamps so that the lighting is very
good. Clean windows thoroughly and regularly to allow
natural sunlight into your home. If you wash your windows with white vinegar, it is not only a natural cleaner
that doesn't leave poisonous residue for children or pets,
but it also blesses your home. Open windows when
they are in the direction of lush plants or slow-moving
water. Both these activities are deep sources of positive
chi. Harmonious sounds are good feng shui, so when
rain is tapping on your roof, consider silencing all noise-
making things in your home so you can soak in the
music of nature. One possible origin for the word "window" is "wind's eye." Keep windows closed on a windy
day or when the sights outside your window constitute
what is known as a "poisoned arrow."

An important principle of feng shui is the avoidance of
this poisoned arrow, or *shar*. A poisoned arrow can be many
things, some of which may add to your clutter. Exceedingly
pointy objects are considered to be poisoned arrows. For
example, a CD stand in the middle of a room or a couple of
bookcases sandwiched back to back showing their angles,
an abstract sculpture with a sharp top, a miniature house
with a pointed roof, or a folded-up exercise machine that

looks lonely and out of place. Look at your clutter and find some objects that could be considered poisoned arrows. Anything that has harsh edges and sticks out like a sore thumb could be a poisoned arrow you can clear out of your life. Modern art and weapons displays fit into this category unless they truly soothe your mind. In general, try to balance out any jagged and pointy things, which traditionally represent masculine yang energy, with rounded and wavy things, which represent the feminine yin energy. If you have too many pointed and sharp-edged things, start downsizing by getting rid of them first.

Lucky numbers of objects on display are important. For example, if you have potted plants lined up in a row, make it a lucky number of plants. Strive to make this true of any decorations, curios, or displayed collections you have. Five is an unlucky number, representing chaos and misfortune. If you have five display items, consider getting rid of one of them to make four, which is a number relating to love and education. Two is an unlucky number, representing poor health. If you have two display items, consider clearing that clutter altogether, because if you leave only one it could stick out like a poisoned arrow. Don't leave chairs in odd numbers like five or three. Consider reducing the number of chairs to four or two, respectively. The Chinese believe that happiness comes in pairs. The exception to this is that an odd number of pets may be considered good luck, so keep that in mind before adding a new pet to your home.

The entrance to your home is extremely important in feng shui, because this is how the good chi enters your life. Think of making space for good energy to move. Thus, the entryway should be entirely free of clutter. An entryway that is narrowed or restricted due to clutter will stop up the flow of *chi*. It's especially important to have bright lighting in the entryway. If there are two entry ways to your home, strive to only use one of them or to make one the main entrance so chi does not leak out the other way. Get rid of any clocks that are visible when you first enter your home— you don't want to suggest to visitors that it may be time to leave already. The door to your house should remain closed when not in use to keep the energy from leaking out of your home, especially if you don't own a house but would like to someday.

Do not have a game room or spare room within sight of the front door, as this chi discourages guests from staying or taking you seriously. If you have what you call a "junk room," "mud room," or "rumpus room," clear out any clutter and rename the room. The names alone can be bad feng shui, as they represent clutter or conflict. Consider reframing rooms like this as a study, a den, sunroom, and so on.

The kitchen represents prosperity in feng shui, so counters should be clear. The stove top especially, should not be used as storage. In other magical traditions, the fireplace hearth is the center of the home, so if you own a fireplace you should regularly clear it of ash and charred wood. The ideal kitchen has plenty of clear space on the countertops and nothing hanging down or obscuring from above. The dining room table should not be in view of the front door, lest your guests eat and run. The kitchen and eating area is very important in feng shui, as these regions of the home represent your finances and wealth. Therefore, a cluttered kitchen and dining room can stop the flow of riches to you and your family. Clear any old photos or portraits of the deceased from your dining area. If you must keep them, move them to the living room area where they are more suited to the *yin* energy there.

You should have plenty of free space to move around in to impress your guests. It is bad feng shui to leave any chairs neglected. If you live alone, take turns with your chairs each time you sit down to eat so you don't always leave some of them unoccupied, as this discourages the energy of guests coming to your home. Feng shui is a good reason to reduce the number of chairs in your home to get rid of clutter and to prevent the problem of bad feng shui from unoccupied chairs. Don't allow rooms to feel too cramped because of excess chairs.

If you have a desk, place it near a wall rather than floating in the middle of the room to lend you stability. For added stability, also make sure your back is facing a window when seated at the desk. You should also be able to see the entrance to the room from your desk to avoid others potentially "stabbing" your energy in the back. Take care that an exposed beam does not lie directly over your head when you are seated at the desk, as this could be a poisoned arrow. Also take care that any sharp angles on furniture and other poisoned arrows are not pointing your way while you sit at your desk.

Now that you can see how feng shui encourages clearing clutter, you may have to move your desk around to a cleared area to avoid bad chi. And if you're wondering if there are similar applications in other rooms of the house, you'd be correct.

Like a desk, a bed should not be placed under an exposed beam. When lying in it, you should be able to see the bedroom door. The bed should not be lined up with the door, however, because it looks too much like a coffin on display. Also, the head of the bed should not face the door. Occupants of the bed should be able to exit the bed to either side freely without stumbling into furniture or clutter, allowing chi to flow freely. If you want to attract a love partner, it is especially important to "clear the way." The ideal bed position is with the headboard against the wall and close to the corner diagonally opposite the door.

Mirrors should be removed from the sight of any beds unless they are necessary for the bed occupants to be able to see the door. Also, there should be no photos of people except photos of a current relationship. Obviously you wouldn't want your mom staring down on you while you have sex; it makes for odd energy! For the same reason, religious figures are discouraged unless you associate them with sex or fertility, and childhood toys should also be cleared from the bedroom. Don't keep your exercise equipment there, and if it's there because you don't use it, consider this a good chance to donate it to somebody who will.

Any distractions that suggest activity should be cleared from the bedroom. When you open your eyes in the morning, you should not be able to see any clutter from the bed that might remind you of unfinished work such as a vacuum, a pile of laundry that needs to be washed or folded, or files from work.

Don't use the bedroom as a storage area, or the clutter might negatively affect your intimate relationships. There should be absolutely no clutter underneath the bed and if possible, there should be nothing but empty space there that is regularly swept or vacuumed to allow smooth movement of chi. The only time you should not continuously clean dust from under your bed is when conceiving children and when the pregnant mother is in the bed, as the spirits of potential children may hide in the dust. Mattresses should ideally be turned during the waning of the moon; some people believe the moon's pull will help them stay flat.

Bathrooms should be modest and not call attention to themselves with excess decorations or furnishings. Keep the toilet lid closed to avoid flushing away your wealth, and keep the door to the bathroom closed when not in use.

Your home should always be in good working order to support positive feng shui. You should not have any stuck drawers, peeling paint, burned-out lightbulbs or, worst of all, stuck doors in your home. If your front door sticks when opening, this is especially bad feng shui that should be fixed right away. Fix any cracks in the walls, as they may allow chi to leak from your home.

Care for your home and clear the clutter to allow chi to flow freely. Even your garden and yard should not be cluttered. Clear all weeds and have any stumps or jutting rocks removed to allow the flow of *chi* without any poisoned arrows. If your house is covered too thoroughly with a creeping vine like ivy, clear it. Keep the garden spacious. Leaving parts of your yard or garden empty of cultivation is okay, as this represents an offering of the space back to the nature from which you accepted your gardening space.

Shiny things are good feng shui, which is why you need clean windows and good lighting. Dust your lightbulbs and lamp shades. Keep any smooth surfaces such as counters and tables free of clutter and shine the surfaces frequently. A little bit of furniture polish can go a long way with improving your feng shui.

In general, houseplants are a good thing. However, any poisonous plants may be bad energetically and should be removed. Some popular pretty house plants are poisonous, such as Dieffenbachia, sometimes called the Mother-in-law plant or dumb cane. Don't put a cactus in the bedroom unless you purposely want to reduce your libido. In Hawaiian culture, the ti or ki plant (*Cordyline fruticosa*) may have strong violent energy associated with the volcano goddess Pele when it is red; some may choose to clear it from their homes, but others take their chances with the good luck it may provide.

Although not usually considered part of a house, the garden should be uncluttered. Dead leaves or overgrown weeds can represent a lack of potential or an opportunity that has been missed. Plants that stick out in the garden can be poisoned arrows, and of course you don't want growing plants to narrow the path to your front door.

....

Clearing-Clutter Tip: Whenever I'm clearing clutter and cleaning behind things that haven't been moved in a while, I stir up plenty of spiders. If and when you find them, don't kill them!

In fact, as Tess Whitehurst writes in *Magical Housekeeping*, lore says that a spider will answer a question for you within a week if you whisper it to the spider before releasing it outside.

Perhaps you can ask questions about how to best clear the clutter from your life and wait for the answer to come to you in your dreams or as you begin your clearing work.

....

Creating Sacred Spaces

Arranging things in a pleasing manner is one of the important steps to creating harmony in your home. Now that you've decided what to keep in your life as part of the simplification process, you have to actually use those things. For example, if you kept a good china set from your grandmother, don't just store all those valuable plates in a drawer. Use them. If they break, at least they were broken in the course of being used and enjoyed by your family. Likewise, some of your more beautiful curios, jewels, photographs, statues, and other decorations should be on display to be used and enjoyed. You should have space on shelves, end tables, or cabinets to create small sacred spaces, or display collections that feed your spirit.

Try creating an ancestral sacred space to display framed photos of deceased loved ones you've kept. This sacred space can also display any jewelry or other keepsakes you've kept from your loved ones. Anything you don't have room to display or enjoy should be graciously donated to clear your clutter. Choose a decorative bowl or cup you already own to act as a vessel to hold water as a symbolic offering to your ancestors.

An elemental altar can help establish balance in your household. The four alchemical elements were once thought to make up everything in the universe. By displaying representations of the four elements in your home, you can project your intentions to keep harmony and not clutter up your life with one thing over all of the others. Don't acquire new stuff for your elemental sacred space. The point is not to increase clutter but to attractively display the things you already have. Every object fits into at least one of the four elements, which is the ultimate goal.

On your elemental sacred space, objects facing north should represent the element of earth. A decorative bowl or cup of salt could be there, as could any beautiful crystals, jewels, or other stones you have saved. Green objects can also represent earth. The direction of east represents the element of air and the color yellow. If you have an incense burner, this is a good place to put it. To represent air on my elemental altar, I also have a vase filled with beautiful feathers I've collected. Take caution here, as some people believe feathers kept in the home are bad luck. Next, south represents fire and the color is red, so this direction is great for any candles you've been saving. Finally, the west represents water and the color blue. You can place a decorative bowl or bottle of water there.

If you believe in/worship a higher power, you can also build a sacred space to your deity or altars to the deities of your choice. This is where statues and art can go. Here too you can place incense or plates for offerings. If there are objects that represent the loves or virtues of your idea of divinity, they can be placed here to remind you that these values are always with you. If you have a large home, you may make a clearing clutter project out of turning an entire room into a spiritual room. I am fortunate enough to have a temple room in my house, and I find it very peaceful to be able to retreat to that clutter-free room to meditate at a moment's notice.

....

Clearing-Clutter Tip: Some cultures personify the positive energy of a home's elements and the ease of housekeeping into fairies. Different types of fairies are sometimes called ban-tighes, brownies, chi spirits, cottagers, drakes, and barbados, among many other names in many cultures around the world.

Legend has it that they help keep your home clean at night while you sleep. To attract them, keep your home tidy and welcoming, especially your hearth, if you have one.

Clear especially any clutter made of iron. Place an offering at your hearth of fresh cakes and honey, preferably placed by the woman of the household. You're welcome to eat what's left for breakfast in the morning.

....

Ritual for Blessing a New Home

When blessing a new home, clean the home from top to bottom first, and perform a purification ritual as needed, (see page 65 for an example). Remember to buy new brooms and dishrags for your new house so you don't bring dirt from those objects from your old home into the new. Purchase a bottle of wine or beer that will be consumed only when you sell and leave this new home, when it becomes your old home. Hide it in the back of the cupboards where nobody will accidentally drink it.

Open all your windows and doors to invite blessings. Add a bit of salt to water and sprinkle it in every room of the home. Next, waft incense in each room of the house. Exceptionally good incenses for a new home blessing are frankincense or white sage, though you can find other options in chapter 4 if neither are available. You can say a few words, if you wish. For example:

> Bless this home from roof to floor,
> Bless this home from wall to wall.
> Bless this home from window to door.
> A home that's clutter-free for all.

The burning incense, salt, and water together represent harmony of the four elements. Together, they draw in positive blessings from all directions. If you want to attract money and wealth to the household, you could hide a penny or other small coin in some unseen corner in each room of the house. Of course, do this only if you don't have small children or pets that could eat the pennies. Otherwise, temporarily place a penny in each room during the blessing with incense and salted water, and then remove them when you are finished and donate them to charity.

Your Body:
Simplify, Harmonize, and Reflect

Clutter can affect the body in many ways. Certainly, viewing physical clutter can cause stress, especially if you have no clutter-free place to relax after working hard. However, there is more metaphorical clutter that may need to be cleared from your life. A life with no time for sleep or exercise is a cluttered one. Clearing out your body clutter will be a lot more challenging than clearing the physical clutter from your home, since you can't just bag it up and haul it away. Instead, you'll have to make some serious lifestyle changes, placing a limit on how drastic your simplification stage can be, since what you do will continue for a long time rather than a chore that shows results after a day.

Before getting started on clearing body clutter, I want you to think about what resources you have in life and how ready you are for change. Of course, there's never a *perfect* time completely free of stress. You can't say "Oh, I'll wait before going on a diet until I'm not so busy at work." However, you can decide how drastic your life changes will be. If you have a big support network of friends and family, a relatively stable income, and aren't struggling with chronic illness, you can change a lot of things in your life all at once without fretting at the upheaval and ending up quitting. However, if you're a single mom of five kids working two jobs, try taking baby steps and making only one of these lifestyle changes at a time so you aren't overwhelmed. You'll be dealing with your physical health during this stage of clearing clutter, so consult with your doctor before starting diet and exercise programs if you have any health questions at all. I'll be digging deep into my Bachelor of Science degree in nutrition, anatomy, and physiology training to share with you some basic science and spirit of clearing body clutter.

Step 1: Simplify

Before anything else, simplify your nutrition intake. You can't add on exercise before getting a handle on how much fuel you are consuming and simplifying your meals. To do this, you'll have to count calories, which are a unit for measuring energy expenditure. Foods don't "have" calories; caloric content actually measures the amount of fuel needed to make your body move and perform all the miraculous functions it does every day. Calories are not the same as chi, so you can't really consume metaphysical energy to power your physical body (people have tried and failed). There are techniques for nourishing your metaphysical energy later in this chapter in the section about spiritual fasting so you can use them in conjunction with a healthy diet if you wish.

The simplest form of nourishing yourself is to make sure your body is in a healthy state of homeostasis, a point where you are not only healthy but the calories you take in roughly equal the calories you spend. And you won't know how many calories you take in unless you count them. Do it in whatever way is simplest for you. For some people, it may be adding up calories by hand on a piece of paper. I use an application on my smartphone and a website that does all the math for me. If you need to lose weight, the calories you eat should be less than what you spend. If you need to gain weight or want to build more muscle for strength, the calories you eat will exceed those you spend. You can also use the Internet to calculate your ideal daily expenditure, or visit your doctor if you would like the most accurate estimate that takes into account any special health needs or conditions you may have.

Here's the real trick to simplifying your nutrition: It doesn't matter as much what you eat as long as you consume the appropriate number of calories for you. Some people choose to simplify their diets by eating a vegan, plant-based diet. Some people choose to simplify by eating raw, living foods only. Some people join the hundred-mile movement, and eat all foods grown or raised within a hundred miles of their homes to reduce environmental impact. Some people simplify their diets by eating only organically grown foods. Others strive to conform to what they consider "clean eating," meaning foods that are not processed. There are many other ways to simplify your diet by cutting things out that you think clutter up your body, and I'm not going to recommend one over the other, because that's an individual health decision for you to make (with a nutritionist if needed). For me personally, a vegetarian diet keeps things simple, but for someone else who raises chickens and follows family recipes, a vegetarian diet would be a drastic change that would complicate life considerably.

Simplifying your nutritional intake takes a long time, so you'll start the harmonizing step while you're still getting the hang of simplifying. It's okay to cheat on your simplification sometimes, because the whole point of living healthy and removing body clutter is so that you can have room in your life to splurge and treat yourself with things you like. However, keep these as rare deviations from the norm to maintain your newly simplified lifestyle so you can properly evaluate it during the reflection phase. Your simplification may take place all at once with a drastic pantry and refrigerator cleaning—if you have enough resources to do so—or you might take baby step; for example, cut sugary beverages from your diet. Move toward the goal of only having healthy snacks and meals available at home and work unless your special treats are planned into your meals with careful calorie accounting. Of course you can still let your mom bake you her famous cookies for your birthday, and you can share a cultural treat served by a friend when you're out at a restaurant. You'll enjoy these delicious things even more if you keep them special.

Step 2: Harmonize

Make sure you've got your nutrition simplification under control before moving on to the harmonizing step. Of course, we've been talking about a lifestyle change, so you may still be tweaking your diet and getting used to a healthier life. I only mean that you should think about simplifying without moving on if you feel caught in the confusion of dietary change. If you find yourself constantly struggling with willpower or are otherwise unhappy with the simple diet you've chosen, these are signs that your simplification process is going haywire—you may need to back up a bit and take smaller steps, thinking things through before going through another cycle of simplification.

Lacking willpower and being unhappy with a diet can be markers for eating disorders; other mental or physical restrictions can prevent people from eating what is best for them. I am not a dietician or nutritionist, but I wholeheartedly recommend creating an eating plan and running it by a professional, preferably a doctor, especially if you are already taking any kind of medicine or are on any sort of program. Ideally, you'll know you're on the right track and ready to progress if your changes leave you feeling energized, motivated, encouraged, and healthy.

Now it's time to work on adding some more movement to your life. It may seem counterintuitive to add exercise to a busy life to clear clutter. Believe me, I know. I never played sports when I was young, aside from some brief fun with downhill skiing and pole-vaulting. As a young adult, I figured I was too busy for exercise. I turned to movement and exercise finally out of desperation when I was a school teacher. I had so much clutter in my life at that point, not only material in my home and classroom, but mental clutter as well—I always had work on my plate and felt compelled to do it because it was for the children. I was desperate to have even one hour out of the day where I could choose to *not* think about work and still feel guilt-free. Exercise was the answer. Now, the busier my life gets, the more I know that I need to carve out time to exercise, otherwise my whole life might become cluttered with things unimportant to me. After all, health is on my list of valuable things I am retaining when clearing the clutter from my life.

Anything that moves your body is a good thing. Weight lifting or any sport or activity that makes you lift weights or your body weight will help you become stronger. Cardiovascular exercise or any activity that gets your heart pumping for minutes on end will help you increase your calorie expenditure and raise your endurance and energy. If you're just starting out with vigorous exercise, aim for just twenty minutes three days a week. Increase time and number of days per week gradually from there. If you jump in too enthusiastically, you might injure yourself, which just means spending more time sitting around getting better. Put important exercise time on your calendar so it doesn't get left out of a busy day. For some people, taking a class might be the way to make sure you don't skip it. If you pay money, it's a specific time on your calendar, and you also have people who might be wondering where you are if you skip class that day, so you may be more likely to stick with it. For others, flexibility on the calendar may be key, so picking a workout DVD or a run that can slip in anywhere in the day might be best. Just get moving and keep moving.

Step 3: Reflect

What did you notice about your body clutter clearing? What was easy and what was most challenging? Hopefully you've started to notice some of the benefits of what you're doing. If so, keep doing what you're doing and you'll keep noticing positive changes as the months roll by. If you're finding something too difficult, it may be that you are doing too much and need to scale things back. When I first started running, I found myself frustrated that I couldn't keep up with even the simplest plan designed for a couch potato. After quitting and restarting twice, I realized the problem: even though my plan was sound, I was running too fast and getting too tired to follow the prescribed exercise. After slowing my pace significantly, I was able to follow the plan comfortably. Only after I completed my initial conditioning and training was I able to increase my running speed. Even if you have to take things slow, celebrate your achievements, because this can give you the motivation to progress. The better you feel, the more you will be able to do.

....

Clearing-Clutter Tip: Take a cleansing bath. An herbal bath can be a special treat for yourself as well as a way to cleanse yourself physically and emotionally.

Try a twenty-minute bath with 2 cups Epsom salts, ¾ cup sea salt, and ½ cup baking soda. Adding herbs or essential oils to the water such as lavender, mint, or rosemary can lend a spiritual quality to your bath and may increase your bath's efficacy at clearing your body clutter.

Try holding a bowl of water outside at night so it shows you the reflection of the full moon. Then pour that water into your bath for the purity of the white moon.

A bath on Saturday may be especially helpful for clearing clutter from your body, mind, and spirit because Saturday is associated with the planetary mythology of Saturn, the necessary destruction that precedes new life and creation.

....

In the particular case of those who are cutting calories, you might find that something seems missing in your life when you cut out all of the food you love and focus on throughout your day. This could be a clue that you should focus more on spirit during the next harmonizing portion of your simplifying, harmonizing, and reflecting cycle. If you wake up for a midnight snack, could it be that perhaps you're really waking up for a chat with God? If you're obsessing over what food you want to eat beyond basic calorie needs, perhaps you need to seek deeper meaning in other areas of life that will occupy your mind and feed your spirit.

Intuitive Eating

When you were born, you were gifted with the ability to know when you feel full, satiated, and hungry. Intuitive eating is using the natural methods your body has of knowing what it needs. Though it's not as effective for weight loss as calorie counting and is not a treatment for an eating disorder, intuitive eating is a perfect way to keep nutrition free of confusion and clutter for those who are already at a healthy weight. Rather than watching the clock and stressing about specific meal times and quantities, you can follow your body's cues. Life becomes a whole lot more simple if you make eating as easy as it is for woodland creatures.

To start, ask yourself what it feels like when you are hungry. You could try an experiment where you allow yourself to become truly hungry before eating. Don't get to the point of starving, but you should be hungry enough that you are aware of your need for food. Try this experiment on a normal day or even a busy one. Hopefully food access isn't unreliable for you; you can trust that the universe will present you with an opportunity to reach your fridge or stop by a restaurant or cafeteria when needed. If you're out of touch with your hunger, you may actually have to meditate on your body sensations rather than watching the clock. What does hunger feel like for you? Does it feel like an empty or odd feeling in your stomach? Do you feel your hunger in your head first? Do you notice it as a drop in your energy levels or the edge of a grumpy feeling in your emotional state of well-being? Does your stomach growl when you're starting to get hungry or only when you're truly ravenous? Don't wait too long, or you may have trouble controlling the amount of food you eat, not to mention the drop in your blood sugar levels. If you're not sure whether you're hungry or not, think about whether you could be easily distracted by a phone call from a friend or if you'd have to excuse yourself to eat.

Once you're hungry, get yourself some food in a timely manner. Think about what you would prefer out of every food available to you at the moment. Savory or sweet? What food textures would feel right to you right now? Would you like hot or cool food? Choose what you would like to eat without judging the nutritional or caloric content for this experiment. Serve yourself a small portion, as you can always get more if you want more. Some people use small plates and forks to trick the mind into thinking there's more if they're trying to reduce portions. Consider a small ritual such as lighting a candle or saying grace before your meal, as this way of making meal time special may actually make your food taste better.

Eat slowly and mindfully. Enjoy your food. Eat your favorite part of the meal first instead of choking down your least favorite or a filling side first. It may be hard to slow down if you're used to rushed eating, so try chewing your bites longer and taking a sip of water between each bite. Really savor your food choice and allow yourself to be grateful. Notice the first potential signs of fullness. You may notice that the flavor seems to change, making the food not as delicious as it was when you started your meal. You may notice a gentle heavy feeling in your stomach and a relaxed frame of mind. As soon as you suspect that you might be getting full, slow down even more. Drink your water and chat with others if you are dining with company. If you confirm that you're not hungry by waiting a few minutes, pack away your food to save for later. In some cultures it is good luck to leave a bit of food on your plate, as it represents giving back to spirit or to one's ancestors in gratitude. This practice supposedly assures you'll never go hungry. Remember that food beyond what your body needs to eat is waste, whether it's in the garbage or turned into flab on your body.

If intuitive eating works for you, you can use this as a lifestyle rather than eating meals by the clock. Simply allow yourself access to your favorite foods when you feel like eating them and stop as soon as your hunger is sated. If you need to eat with others, at dinner for example, a shot of orange juice may stave off your hunger long enough. Or instead of eating lunch at a restaurant with friends, if you ate earlier you can enjoy a glass of water and good conversation. While experimenting in this way, you may wish to use only water or other calorie-free drinks you have on hand until you get a good feel for how caloric beverages affect your hunger. It can be trickier to know whether you are getting hungry or getting full if you're drinking milk, juice, or soda with your meals. Keep it simple.

Fasting

Fasting is a spiritual practice that spans many different faiths as part of their spiritual practice. It may have risen independently in many cultures as a way to clear body clutter and press the body's reset button. Specifically, there are a number of spiritual benefits to fasting that may allow you to harmonize that part of your life.

During a fast, abstaining from eating food can help remind you that your focus is on the spiritual part of life instead of the physical. It's like tying a string around your finger to remember something, only much more persistent. Undertaking a fast may produce the light-headed state associated with trance meditation, a state of mind that's potent and powerful for prayer and other spiritual practices. Also, fasting allows you to put energy into your spiritual focus and spiritual work that you would otherwise spend seeking, preparing, and digesting food. Some people even take the opportunity during fasting to give the resources they would have consumed to others who are less fortunate.

Depending on your health needs, a fast can take different forms (it isn't just starving yourself for a period) so consult your doctor if you have any questions. Every religion in which fasting is a practice allows exemptions for the disabled, women who are pregnant or nursing, children, the elderly, and those who need a lot of calories to perform their work. Some fasts can be very short, lasting for one day and ending at sundown. Other fasts simply exclude certain foods such as meat, or they limit caloric consumption to liquids like juice. I like to do a juice fast during the day of a full moon. It helps me clear my mind and focus on the right things in life. If you're healthy enough to try a fast and you think it may be for you, give it a try.

....

Clearing-Clutter Tip: Calories are not the same as spiritual energy, but here's a meditation that you can use to draw in spiritual energy whether you're temporarily fasting or simply feel like you need some intangible nourishment. Use this when you feel like eating out of boredom or emotional unrest.

Sit and take deep breaths. As you inhale, think of yourself as a being made entirely of loving energy. Imagine that you are breathing in through your chest through an energy center right at your heart.

As you exhale, imagine you are radiating love in every direction through your body. Tell yourself that everything you need to be healthy and strong and a positive presence in the world comes to you through the air you breathe and the spiritual energy that comes with it.

....

Mindful Exercise

When most people think about mindful exercise, they might think about yoga, Tai Chi, and other martial arts or spiritual dance. Mindful exercise doesn't have to be something traditionally associated with the spiritual, however. Any physical discipline will do. When I was in college, archery was my sport of choice and a vital touchstone for clearing mental and spiritual clutter. When I toed the line at the archery range and let my eyes focus on the tip of that arrow and the target ahead of me, everything else would disappear. My muscles burned but my mind and body felt clear. My young life's social struggles and homework worries disappeared and the only thing left was the focus.

The first time I turned to more physical exercise was actually when my schedule was more packed, as a school teacher. Every waking moment that I wasn't working, I was thinking about working or planning my work. Any time spent trying to relax or sleep resulted in me feeling guilty that I wasn't doing more work to serve the school and kids entrusted to my service. I volunteered for more work and became a curriculum leader for the district and attended extra classes to extend my learning. Well, my life was packed with way too much mental and physical clutter and my body was totally neglected. Paradoxically, I squeezed one more regular appointment into my schedule: karate classes. For an hour a day I was blissfully able to pay attention only to my strained breathing, form, and the pain of my exertion. I was hooked.

My latest love in mindful exercise is running. Of course, there's nothing inherently spiritual or clutter clearing about running, but I highly recommend it to those physically able to do it. Not only does running not require the extra clutter of equipment for its practice, it can give the same clarity of mind found in other types of mindful exercise. And it's free, to boot. It took me four months of running consistently before I learned not to hate it, but then I grew to love it. Running gives me the time to clear the clutter of my body, mind, and spirit while taking some much needed time for myself.

Making Time for Sleep

Sleep is vital for harmonizing your life. Adults need seven to eight hours of sleep and even more if you're pregnant, breastfeeding, or an athlete. Make a commitment to give your body and mind the right amount of sleep needed to clear out all the clutter of the previous day. Give yourself a proper bedtime and get yourself ready for rest hours before hand. Some people believe that dirty dishes in the sink prevent restful sleep, so build that clearing clutter chore into your bedtime routine. I like to load the dishwasher and turn it on before I go change into my pajamas so I have clean dishes to put away in the morning before breakfast. Power down all screens like televisions or computers a couple hours before bedtime to get your mind ready for sleep. I like to catch up on my reading in bed.

Keep your bedroom for sleeping if your living space allows. Don't put televisions, exercise equipment, or hobbies that excite and engage you too much in there. Exercising in the afternoon or morning may make sleep come easier to you at night. If you can help it, don't exercise right before bed but of course do what you have to with your schedule to fit what you need in your life.

If you're way too ambitious like me, you might feel like you're slacking if you allow yourself extra hours to sleep. But think of it this way: dreaming is a very productive activity— a way to simultaneously clear the clutter of your mind and body. When you dream, your brain processes the activities of the day as well as your intuition about the future. While your body knits wounds, heals illnesses, and restores balance, your mind sorts through your problems and puts memories in their proper emotional place.

To work with your dreams, start by keeping a dream journal. Keep a notebook and writing implement by your bed as well as a small light you can use. Inform anyone sharing the room with you about your dream journal intentions. As soon as you wake up, even if it is nowhere near the time you start your day, write down what you remember about your dream. It may be difficult to force yourself into that level of being awake, especially if you try to write legibly. However, it can be worth it for the insights you receive. Sometimes I don't even remember what I wrote when I wake up the next day.

After keeping your dream journal for a while, you may notice that issues become clearer. You can track your life as it unfurls in your subconscious. If you approach your dream journal with the same discipline used in approaching your material clutter simplification, you will reap benefits.

"Unnecessary possessions are unnecessary burdens. Many lives are cluttered not only with unnecessary possessions but also with meaningless activities. Cluttered lives are out-of-harmony lives and require simplification. Wants and needs can become the same in a human life and, when this is accomplished, there will be a sense of harmony between inner and outer well-being. Such harmony is needful not only in the individual life but in the collective life too."

....

Peace Pilgrim

Three

....

Mental Clutter:
The Past and the Future

Clearing material and body clutter can have a strange effect on your brain. On the one hand, you may find some satisfaction and an immediate sense of relief. Without the various "to do" clutter on your list you may feel a sense of freedom and release from guilt. On the other hand, you may find yourself at loose ends. As you begin to incorporate clearing clutter into your regular life, it no longer seems to be a good excuse for balancing your mental and emotional life. If your house is in order, there's no reason you can't invite friends and relatives over unless there are some other valid issues to address. Mental clutter is a bit more challenging than material clutter; like body clutter, it requires a lifestyle change. Unlike all forms of physical clutter, your very faculty for assessing your problems, your mind, may be the source of your biggest problem. Though clearing mental clutter is no substitute for treating mental illness, it can be a vital part of living a happy life.

Simplify, Harmonize, and Reflect Intellectually

It's time to clear the clutter and cobwebs out of your brain. This process will be different for different people. Some have busy lives that are overscheduled and under-thought. Others may have days and evenings free of work and appointments, and yet might have a mind like a hamster wheel of negative thoughts, worries, and life patterns. Both people could use a break and a means of purging some of that unwanted stress and baggage. Even if some of the tips in this chapter don't apply to you, consider whether you would like to try some of them for clearing mental clutter. Something as simple as a spiritual retreat might be a radical change, like going to a cabin or camping in a remote wooded area; maybe it's more complex, like a complete overhaul of your cluttered life with the knowledge that you can always bring elements into your life as you please. Unlike physical clutter, you don't have to bag up your mental clutter and throw it away for good.

Step 1: Simplify

Assess how radically you need to downsize your mental clutter at this time. If you feel stressed out, like you have no time to think, you may have to do the mental equivalent of clearing out all the clutter in your home and starting over—meditation. Meditation consists of clearing your mind of all thoughts for a set period of time. There is a joke about meditation that starts with a student approaching a meditation teacher and asking him how long she should meditate each day. The teacher replied that the student should meditate at least an hour a day. "A whole hour?" the student exclaims. "I don't have time to meditate for an hour every single day!" The teacher smiles and replies, "In that case, you should meditate for three hours daily."

The joke is funny because meditation is hard. If it was easy, anyone could clear their minds on the spot and mental clutter wouldn't exist. The good news is that with practice, you can become proficient enough that you will be able to meditate even in the middle of a stressful work day or on a crowded bus. More about meditation and techniques will appear later in this chapter, but for now, here's a meditation for the complete beginner.

Your first meditations will not be an hour long. If you're new to this and feeling ambitious, shoot for twenty minutes. And if, like me, you've struggled with attention deficit disorder or just plain distractibility, try for five minutes and lower that time if necessary. My first meditation as a teen must have been about thirty seconds, and my three year old enjoys ten- to twenty-second meditations.

Find a comfortable place where you will not be disturbed. Silence your cell phone and power down any other distracting electronics. Lock doors or put up "do not disturb" signs if necessary. Seat yourself and close your eyes. Attempt to clear your mind of all extraneous thought.

Naturally, thoughts will arise. "What am I going to make for dinner? What time is my appointment tonight?" Observe them as if they are outside of yourself, and let them float away like balloons. Some may find it helpful to focus on a mantra said silently in the head or even out loud, like the phrase "clearing clutter" over and over again. Others may find it helpful to focus on a part of the body, such as the forehead, right between the eyebrows. This location represents the intellect and the higher self, which can keep your focus above earthly matters. Neither of these extra techniques are required, however. It may simply take daily practice over a few months before you settle into and even begin to enjoy the routine.

....

Clearing–Clutter Tip: Does your mind sometimes get so cluttered that you can't remember where you left your car keys or a person's name that's on the tip of your tongue? Here is a simple meditation that can be used to clear your mind in order to recover a memory.

Close your eyes and take a deep breath, drawing out the exhale longer than the inhale. Picture a black door in your mind very clearly. Visualize every detail so vividly that it is as if the door were right in front of you. In your mind's eye, open the door and walk through it.

Now you can open your eyes and continue your day as normal. Don't try to push yourself to remember anything. The wayward memory will pop into your head.

....

Another drastic simplification you may need to do is clearing your schedule. Go on a retreat and declare a personal day if possible. Quit or put on hold as many commitments as possible, keeping in mind that there may be a great many that can be taken up again when you feel ready. Allow yourself the time to relax and even get bored. Consider a "technology fast" where you take a break from all forms of electronic entertainment for a day or a week. Give yourself a sabbat day once a week during which you won't talk on the telephone, use the computer or other devices. If you're not ready for that, try turning off your phone after six o'clock each night so you're not constantly at technology's beck and call.

Step 2: Harmonize

When you allow space in your life for your intellect to blossom and grow, magic happens. You might find that you're quite creative. Abandoned musical and artistic pursuits may call to you. You might feel compelled to call old friends or family members with whom you haven't spoken in a long time. You might feel a tug pulling you toward spiritual or religious study. After you've sat with the "boredom" of cleared mental clutter, follow your whims. This time, however, make sure you don't end up cluttering your life all over again with things that are too stressful and not meaningful to you.

Avoid re-cluttering by remembering your list of what you considered to be most valuable when you were clearing the clutter from your home. If the new activities you're signing up for don't fit in with your deepest values, you shouldn't make room in your life for them. This is especially hard for me, because I love signing up for new things, but am pretty bad at following through for the long haul. Like me, you may have to exercise the tough skill of saying "no" even when it is to people you care about very much. However, when you stick to your list of only the most valuable things in life, you'll find that your life activities seem to hang together in a weirdly synchronistic way. You can put more on your plate because things fit together well on that plate.

Step 3: Reflect

How's that meditation going? Are you able to fit it into your routine? Consistency is key to gain and maintain proficiency in this useful skill. Think about what was most easy and most difficult about your first try at clearing your mental clutter. To what extent were you able to clear your schedule? Are there still things in your life that aren't valuable but you cling to them and continue to put mental effort into them? You may have very important emotional or ethical reasons for doing so, and now is the time to metaphorically and literally meditate on those choices. What follows are some things to ponder and some tips and tricks for clearing mental clutter. As with physical clutter, this cycle of clearing will be ongoing.

Meditation Techniques

You've already tried the simplest form of meditation in chapter 2, on page 38. Other meditation techniques are alluded to in the section in that same chapter on caring for your body. Meditation can certainly help your body and mind by lowering your blood pressure and reducing stress, and it can also be a spiritual practice as well. Letting go of your thoughts in meditation is a gesture of releasing attachments and desires, even if only for a moment. Meditation can also allow you to be receptive to positive thoughts and energies as they come to you from your natural environment, the divine, or fellow people. If you'd like to explore the practice of meditation further, or if you've been struggling and would like other meditation tools in your toolkit, try some of these spiritual meditation techniques.

Breathing meditation

Focusing on breathing can be one way to make meditation much easier. Giving yourself a singular thing to think about in your body can help keep intrusive and distracting thoughts at bay. Breath has always been a metaphor for spirit, and breathing itself is a way you share the element of air with every other person who has ever existed, past and present. Breath itself can also spiritually nourish the body. Here are some more ways you can use breath control to aid and enhance your meditation.

At first, attempt meditation by simply observing your breath, without controlling it. Notice how your breathing slows the longer that you sit in rest. Next, you can try controlling your breathing through a basic technique called square breathing, called so because you breathe in for four counts, hold your breath for four counts, breathe out for four counts, and hold your breath for four counts again. If you try this technique right off the bat, it may feel very difficult; you'll want to gasp for breath. But this is good! The challenge will engage and distract you from thinking too much during meditation.

To make square breathing easier, try choosing counts based on your heart beats. This way, if your heart rate is elevated, you won't be exerting energy unnaturally and feel the need to gasp so much for air. Now try breathing in for four heartbeats, holding your breath for four heartbeats, breathing out for four heartbeats, and then holding your breath again for four heartbeats. If at first this is still too difficult, you can modify it by only holding your breath for two heartbeats.

When you master square breathing, no matter how annoying it may feel in practice, stick with it for a few minutes of meditation. At first, you may have to give it everything you've got. After a few minutes, however, your body will adapt to the pattern and you may find yourself forgetting that you're even doing it. At that point, the relaxing effect will work its magic to slow your heart rate and deepen your meditation perhaps even to the point of trance.

Walking meditation

A walking meditation may appeal to those who are more fidgety. As a person who struggles with attention issues, I certainly find walking meditation to be easier than the seated style. The action of walking replaces breathing or other focii to reduce distracting thoughts. Best of all, if you can perform your walking meditation out in nature, you can commune with creation, Mother Earth, or however else you conceptualize divinity in the natural world.

Choose a safe place for walking meditation that is not near any dangerous traffic. You don't want to have to force your active mind to stay alert. Instead, find some place where you can zone out without any fear of being attacked or hit by a car. Begin walking at a brisk pace. If you can get your heart rate elevated during this meditation, so much the better, as you can rely on endorphins in your body to help you achieve a trance state. Focus on your footfalls hitting the ground and try to think of nothing else. As a runner, I meditate while running and find some amazing benefits: the thoughts that do creep into my meditations are positive ones. My focus begins to sharpen on moments of beauty. I'll hear a bird's song, see a beautiful mushroom, smell fabulous food on a barbecue, or hear a child practicing a musical instrument in a nearby home. By the time I'm finished with my run, my mind is empty of my worldly worries and cares, and I've accumulated hundreds of new moments of beauty I can cherish forever.

Psychic meditation

Meditation can be used to attune with your psychic self. "Psychic" here refers to the intuitive senses inherent in all people that cannot necessarily be attributed to the usual five senses. Psychic does not mean omniscient. In fact, everyone is at least a little bit psychic. Meditation can be one way to receive psychic messages from your inner self, the universe at large, from the divine, or from wherever else you think such wisdom might originate.

Before your psychic meditation practice, make sure you have a pen and paper handy to write down any insights that come to you. You may also wish to select a topic, like love or career. Or, you can choose a question on which to focus. To practice psychic meditation, you should work especially hard to eliminate all distractions; there won't be any walking meditation for this one at first. Make sure you silence any electronics and lock any doors that might disturb you during your meditation. Sit in silent, receptive meditation and clear your mind. Try not to distract yourself, even by focusing on your breathing. If you must aid yourself with a focus, turn your attention to your solar plexus or navel, the area believed to be the home of an energy center you use to psychically observe your surroundings naturally at all times. Conversely, you could focus on your topic or question, driving all other thoughts from your mind.

Wait for psychic messages to come to you. Time your meditation with a timer that will chime at the end of your session, and stretch your meditation to the limits of what you can stand. At the end of your meditation, record any thoughts or insights you can recall, even if they don't seem to be anything important. Some intuitive thoughts that come to you during psychic meditation may seem like riddles and could make more sense later on. Through experience, you can learn to interpret your psychic meditative thoughts.

Mantra meditation

Another way to make meditation feel easier is selecting a mantra. A mantra is a repeated phrase or affirmation that you can speak aloud or think in your head, depending on your preference. Saying a mantra, especially one you can say while breathing in and out, can be a way to make the meditation time seem to move faster and it maintains a singular focus for the duration of your meditation. Your mantra can be a prayer like, "Let all I do serve God," or it can be an affirmation of what you want such as, "Clutter be gone." A prayer-style meditation can be helpful if you want your life and actions to become more spiritual. An affirmation can be helpful if you want to take the psychological approach to try to change your habits into whatever you want.

If possible, I recommend making your own mantra. That way, there will be no question that it makes sense to you. You can also tailor your mantra so it will fit into your breathing pattern. An ideal mantra is something you can repeat while you push out air and suck it in. Remember, you're not trying to communicate the phrase to another person; it doesn't matter if you sound funny while you're gasping and speaking at the same time. The point is that you can speak comfortably whether at a murmured whisper or singing a song. Try creating your own pair of mantras, three to six syllables long, one a prayer and one an affirmation. You can string them together if you like.

Practice meditating while speaking your mantra aloud. In one session you can try your mantra at a whisper. In another, you can try speaking your mantra in a monotone. One session could be about trying to set your mantra to a simple tune. And you could also try just thinking your mantra without saying it out loud in another. Take note of how each attempt affects your attention span and your level of happiness. Choose which method of chanting works best for you.

The best thing about making up your own mantras is that you can have a specific mantra for every situation. You can have a mantra for clearing clutter, a mantra for Mondays, a mantra for when you're feeling especially stressed, and a mantra for when you're just feeling thankful to be alive. It might complicate things if you change your mantra too often within meditation sessions, but choosing a new mantra each time you meditate is fine. This new bit of novelty may be the trick to make meditation easier for you.

Peace meditation

Meditation doesn't have to be something that only pertains to your own personal life without impacting others. Ideally, your spiritual practice will positively affect and influence those around you. Meditating on peace can help you in many ways. It can relax you and clear the clutter from your spiritual life, leaving only whatever makes you feel at peace. Secondly, the energies you generate in yourself having to do with peace could possibly inspire or influence those around you, creating a ripple effect of peace. This isn't to say that world peace is a simple accomplishment, of course. You don't have to guilt trip yourself about human nature or quit your martial arts lessons if those give you joy. However, any little bit of peace you can add to the world is good.

Peace starts in the heart of each individual. During meditation, if you can find peace even just for yourself within your soul, you can begin to share peace. The sharing of peace begins with those closest to you, like your children or your spouse. Beyond that, you can share peace as a family with your community, schools, and workplaces. Your communities can then radiate peace to your nation and the world beyond.

To perform a peace meditation, try the following. If you have a white candle on hand, light it. If not, simply visualizing a lit white candle will do just fine. The guru mentioned in the next chapter, Amma, invites everyone on the planet to perform a peace meditation at 7 pm local time to send a wave of peace across the world at any given moment in time. She advises the Sanskrit mantra *Om lokah samastah sukhino bhavantu* (OM loh-KAH sah-mah-STAH soo-kee-NOH bah-VAHN-too), which basically means, "of all the universe, may all the beings everywhere find peace and happiness." Repeat this mantra as long as you can, and then end it with *Om, shanti, shanti, shanti* (OM SHAN-tee, SHAN-tee, SHAN-tee) which basically means "universal peace, peace, peace." Extinguish your candle and go about your evening. This meditation can be done while doing your household chores, or in walking or seated meditation.

Transmission meditation

Transmission meditation is another sort of meditation designed to radiate peace and other great stuff to the rest of humanity. It was invented by a man named Benjamin Crème, who believes that there are many great people on earth who are already working towards peace and clearing clutter from humanity's minds, bodies, and spirits. The idea behind transmission meditation is that you and I can sit in meditation and allow energies to flow from the divine through us to the people already doing good works. It's sort of acting like a battery or a transmitter for activities already in motion. Transmission meditation is delightfully like a spiritual volunteer job for lazy people, allowing anyone to be a link in the chain towards a more utopian existence, or possibly even enlightenment.

Practicing transmission meditation is mercifully simple. The first step is to sit in meditation and clear the mind, as usual, but you get two focus tools to help the job along. First, you can turn your attention to the spot between your eyebrows. This spot is often called the *ajna* or third eye, as it relates to the higher psychic center, associated with the divine rather than just surviving with what intuition you need to use to navigate human interactions. You'll find that your attention naturally drops lower through your body as you get tired and bored. If you find yourself focusing on the navel or solar plexus, snap your attention back up to the third eye.

The next nifty tool that you can use for transmission meditation is to use the simple mantra "om." Om is a word that is supposed to represent the entire universe. If you say it slowly like, "AUM" you will slowly open your mouth into a round shape and then seal your lips in a hum. This is said to mimic the creation of the universe and the eventual inevitable contraction of the universe to nothingness. As such, the "om" sound is a powerful sound because it contains everything that can and will be. You can use this sound to center yourself on the spiritual whenever your attention wanders. You can say "om" out loud, or you can simply think it in your mind without even saying it out loud. You'll notice that the sound naturally draws your attention back up to the third eye where you want it to be. Meditate until your predetermined time is up and you have completed your session. You can practice transmission meditation daily or weekly. Benjamin Crème designed transmission meditation to be performed frequently and in groups of three or more, with a special invocation spoken to encourage the divine to bring positive energies through the meditation.

Overscheduling and Time Thieves

Imagine a big empty jar and next to it is a pile of rocks and sand. Every day, you have to fill this jar with that pile of rocks. If you haphazardly throw the rocks in the jar, many of them won't fit. Instead, you should begin by placing the largest rocks in the bottom. Smaller rocks can fit in between these larger rocks. Sand could easily fill in the smallest gaps. Life is much the same. You can paradoxically get more done if you plan for just a few of the most important things that need to get done in a day. Get those things done, and a wide expanse of time seems to open up for the good and little things.

Life can get cluttered with scheduled events. There may be work, school, exercise, and personal care appointments. If you have kids, you might be shuttling them to sports practice or instrument lessons. The life of the modern family looks very different than it did in the past; there is very little room for boredom. Kids and even adults have no time for unstructured play. Yet, out of boredom comes creativity and the yearning for balance and harmony with your spirituality. An overscheduled life is a cluttered one. I live by my calendar and pride myself on not being flakey—everything that lands on my calendar sticks. I have to be cautious about not adding too many things to my calendar or letting things become unbalanced.

Paradoxically, sometimes adding time on your calendar to complete tasks will help to clear your mind. For example, putting twenty minutes of exercise into your daily planner in the morning is better than rushing to squeeze it in to your evening after everything else has been done. Go ahead and add the chore of taking the trash can to the curb to your calendar. Now you don't have to think about it all day, cluttering your brain with a nagging task.

....

Clearing-Clutter Tip: If you're a visual sort of person, try color coding your day planner or online calendar.

For example, work projects could be green, family appointments pink, medical appointments in blue, leisure time in purple, and so on.

That way, you can quickly see whether your life is getting out of balance or overwhelmed. All free time is not equal.

If you have too much work on your plate and not enough play, you will need to make slight adjustments as time marches on.

....

Give yourself the gift of downtime and even boredom. What about a retreat? Whether a weekend of camping or a stay at a hotel, giving yourself a time away from the usual demands of your schedule can help you gain perspective about what you really want and need. If you can't afford a real retreat, give yourself a virtual retreat by simplifying your schedule down to just the basics. Aside from what you need to keep your family going, cancel all your social obligations and step down from any leadership or hosting positions you don't really need to fill. Those opportunities will still be there later if you decide to add things back into your life. Once you've simplified things down to the basics, it may be easier to determine which things are more important than others. When your plate is too full, everything on your schedule appears (falsely) to be just as important as everything else.

The Right Attitude Toward Life

An attitude adjustment may be in order if you find your mind cluttered with negativity. There was a reason your mother told you that if you have nothing nice to say to say nothing at all. Years ago, I decided to take that advice. Previously, I had thought I was being honest and open by sharing my complaints all the time. Our culture of oversharing and constant social media certainly encourages this. But it turns out that this habit encourages a bad attitude.

After realizing I was just feeding my own negativity, I kept my whining to a minimum. This doesn't mean I never complained again; however, when I spoke about a problem that needed a solution, I allowed my displeasure to be voiced. Perhaps I could get some help solving the problem. But if the problem was unsolvable, permanent, or out of my control, I learned not to give it more power over my life by mentally and verbally obsessing about it. If each of us gave voice to every complaint we had in life, from the grit between our toes to the glare of the sun in the sky, there wouldn't be enough minutes in the day to catalogue all those complaints. So instead, let them go.

Focus on positive thoughts. When you put out positive thoughts and energy into the universe, you will receive that energy in return. At first, you might have to fake it until you make it. Face a person you don't care for and think to yourself, "I like you." Or pick one thing you like about that person if you think saying you like him or her too disingenuous. Force yourself to smile, as the physical act of smiling can actually lift your spirits, even when joy was not there at first. Assume the best of people whenever possible and safe. Seek out the little joys in life and seize them. Enthusiastically blow them out of proportion.

Purify Your Thoughts

Negative thoughts can become somewhat of a lifestyle. My mother taught me this as a child, that thoughts become things. When I would whine that I didn't have any friends at school, she encouraged me not to speak of such things, lest they become a pattern in my life. At the time, being the friendless kid had become a melodramatic identity that felt comfortable. I resisted change because getting rid of those negative thoughts felt like letting go of part of myself. When I did purify myself of those thoughts by replacing them with more positive ones about my character, my fate and friendships changed.

Take a scrub brush to your mind and scour all the negative thought patterns you find there repeating themselves every day. This process might feel difficult. Perhaps you've built an identity around hating your body every time you look in the mirror, for instance. At one point in my life, I had forged my identity around hating myself in every way. Climbing out of that hole felt like a lie at first, but my stubborn insistence on this misplaced "honesty" was just an excuse to wallow in my mental clutter. I didn't have clinical depression forcing my brain to think in those ways, so I was able to turn things around for myself. Here are some tips that worked for me and that might work for you.

Catch yourself when you're thinking negative thoughts. Make note of what precipitates your negative thinking. Maybe you're tired or hungry, or maybe something else triggered your thinking, like seeing an unflattering photo of yourself. If you can do anything about these patterns, change them. Find ways to flatter yourself and take care of your needs so you won't find your thoughts slipping into dark places.

Sometimes, the brain can ruminate over bad things. I might make a big mistake, for instance, and blow things by saying something rude or cruel to my husband. Then I tend to agonize over that mistake long after I've said my apologies. At night, I will replay the conversation over and over in my head, kicking myself for doing the wrong thing. If you find yourself with these repetitive negative thoughts when there's nothing you can do to make the situation better, replace them with positive thoughts. Try using affirmations about what you want to hear. Use the present tense as if you had already achieved what you want. Instead of saying, "I want to be rich," say "I am wealthy." At first, replacing your old narratives with new ones will feel awkward and fake, but once you start catching yourself making the switch smoothly, pat yourself on the back.

Purify Your Desires

You don't have to take a vow of chastity to have pure desires. But you should know your place in the grand scheme of life, and not fight that place so hard that it poisons your life. The mythologist Joseph Campbell wrote about this, saying, "Follow your bliss." If you are on your right path in life, your challenges will seem relatively easy or at least appropriate for you. If you are on the wrong path and not following your true pure and highest ideals, even the simplest troubles will seem insurmountable.

Let me illustrate this with an example. When I had a job I hated with an hour-long commute, I suffered through the daily drive. I sighed noisily at red lights and I swore at other drivers. I gritted my teeth and my blood pressure must have been through the roof. But when I had a three-hour commute to a job I loved, the drive was entirely different. I turned on the radio and sang out loud. My trip through the countryside was a time for me to relax and prepare for the work ahead. It seemed like nothing to me, and I was genuinely surprised when others said they could never handle the same commute on a regular basis. I was following my bliss. Look back to your list of the most valuable things in your life to see some of your purest desires, or explore more of your spirituality in chapter 4 to discover new, pure desires. Cut impure desires out of your life ruthlessly.

Happiness is a measure of your appreciation for what you have versus your desires. If you could write out an equation for happiness, it would look like this:

$$Happiness = Appreciation \div Desire$$

To acquire more happiness, you can either increase your appreciation for what you already have or decrease your level of desire for what you don't have. You'll have to take a hard look at your individual situation to find out what is going on. If your mind is cluttered with desires large and small, you might have to purge some of them. One clue that this is the case is when all your desires seem equal in strength. If getting a new pair of shoes seems as important in the moment as taking care of your health, you'll need to purge the irrational fixation.

Purify Your Motives

Imagine your life is a series of cups labeled with different things that motivate you. One cup might say "career" and another might read "family." Now imagine you also have a vessel filled with oil. Every time you pour the oil from one cup to another, you lose a little as it clings to the walls of the cup. That is, you use up the inner resources you have in life when you switch from one extrinsic motivation to another. Spiritual people try to be motivated by spirit, because spirit is a sort of magical cup that never needs to be replenished.

Motivation is different from desire. If your desire is a stable house and home, for example, you might be motivated by an impure motive like greed, or by a more pure motive such as harmony with family members and having enough (with some to spare to give away to those who do not). Motives are tricky to separate from desires because our culture has specific tracks that you are supposed to follow to get what you are supposed to desire. We're told to grow up, get a job, get married, and have children. If you feel unhappy after failing to complete one or more of those tasks—or worse, after dutifully accomplishing all of them— you will feel rightfully confused about your motivations. We all know that single people are not "incomplete" and can be just as happy as people who choose to build a family.

But talking about happiness is where things start to get abstract and maybe uncomfortable for those who like to map out life in simple steps. Purifying your motivations means clinging to those highest desires and letting go of your fixation on how they will be achieved. Pay attention to how you may be wishing, hoping, or praying to see how to streamline and purify your motivations. Let's say you find yourself thinking, "I hope my boss lets my paycheck come through a couple days early this month so I can get my car out of the shop." Replace this with, "I have safe and reliable transportation anywhere I need to go." The new statement

is in present tense, as recommended earlier. Most importantly, it releases the manner in which you receive what
you need. A friend might come in town and lend you a car.
You might win a class action legal suit you never knew you
entered and receive a settlement. Your next-door neighbor
might get a job at your workplace and offer to carpool. Your
motivations are transmuted from anxiety and fear to faith
and your true desires.

Letting Go of Envy, Jealousy

"Comparison is the thief of joy," Teddy Roosevelt once
said. Envy can be a subtle enemy; you don't have to gawk
at celebrity wardrobes to be its victim. Instead, envy can
be borne out of a lack of self-esteem such as wondering
if you're doing as well by your children as some other
mother or father out there. In other words, admiring others can turn to envy if you put yourself down in the process. Letting go of envy means boosting your self-esteem,
which is the same technique for clearing the mental clutter of jealousy.

Jealousy is rooted in the fear of not being good enough
for a significant other, friendship, or even a relative. A related problem is a reliance on external validation from
somebody else who is important to you. For some people,
this can be pretty intense. As a young adult, I was devastated any time my parents or my significant other felt
angry or sad and would immediately blame myself. Eventually, I had to seek my own internal validation because

I cannot force somebody else to feel a certain way about me or anyone else. All I can do is work to clear my own cluttered emotions.

Self-esteem takes time to build, but the good news is that once it is established, many cluttered thoughts will melt away. To build your self-esteem, turn inward for validation whenever possible. If you find yourself reaching out to a friend or a lover to make everything all better, stop yourself. Instead of asking someone else whether something is okay or looking to examples of others, pay attention to your own core values. If you don't quite match up to what you want to be, that's no reason to beat yourself up. Rationally, you know that negative self-talk won't get you any closer to your goals. You'll need to either readjust your expectations or simply keep doing the best you're able. Just like a physical fitness plan, your self-esteem "fitness" will take time to form. You can't break all your bad habits overnight but you can slowly reduce their occurrence. I had such low self-esteem when I was a school teacher that I would actually schedule thirty minutes into my daily appointment book to cry. Yes, that's right, I allotted time to feel sorry for myself and cry over all the mistakes I had made. That way, it was actually a blessing if I didn't have to use those thirty minutes.

Releasing Worry

Worry is worthless. True concerns are different from worries, as being concerned about something implies there is a way to change or fix it. Worry is a useless exercise you put your brain through when nothing can be done about a situation, and those mental gymnastics can actually be harmful. Here's an interesting trick I learned from palmistry or fortune-telling using the hands. Take a look at your dominant hand on the fleshy part of your palm at the base of your thumb. You may see many small lines radiating from your thumb. Those are worry lines, and legend says the more worry lines you have, the more of a worry-wart you are. If those lines cross your life line, the line that curves across your palm, it means your worries are affecting your health and longevity.

Whether or not the palmistry is true, we all know that constant stress can affect mental and physical health. Releasing worry can be a difficult thing to do, however. Happily, there are many effective strategies. Simplification of your life is one way. This may require delegating your worries to other people who can take action regarding those worries, turning them into concerns. Some people delegate their worries to God, and giving worries up to the divine is the ultimate expression of faith. For others not willing or able to take that step, simply distracting the self from worries until such time as ignoring worry becomes habit may have to suffice.

Reacting to Criticism

I seem to attract people into my life who are great at over-reacting to criticism. My father was a perennial blame-shifter, which led to my own aversion to accepting blame.

I would turn into a giant diva whenever criticism came my way. My husband is a perfectionist who avoids starting anything about which he might get criticism. And now I have two young children who might very well dissolve into tears if I use anything less than a cheery tone. Why do we all clutter up even constructive criticism with all these feelings and aversions to change?

Part of the reason may be self-esteem, which you could be working on already. Once you have a high enough self-esteem, criticism will seem less like a reason for sadness and more as an opportunity to better yourself. Paradoxically, an over-inflated ego can also hamper appropriate response to criticism, as it may feel like everyone is attacking you with bogus claims. It is challenging to find that sweet spot where you know yourself but are also willing to change.

The best way to react to criticism is to detach the actual critique from the person delivering the message to you. Evaluate it objectively without immediately reacting. Sometimes, even a wildly bogus assertion may have some nugget of truth in it you can use for self-improvement. Give yourself some time to objectively consider the criticism after you have time to separate the criticism from any social situation in which you may have received the feedback.

....

Clearing-Clutter Tip: Try these steps to clear conflict, modeled after the Baha'i faith practice called "consultation."

1. Gather all conflicted parties together.

2. If appropriate, begin the meeting with a prayer for all to go well and to establish a goodwill atmosphere of a community coming together to help each other for the good of all.

3. Lay out all of the facts of the matter. Try to remove judgment and speculation, although the way someone feels can count as a fact.

4. Encourage everyone present to offer solutions. As each solution is offered, all should release ownership of the idea.

5. Strive for consensus on a solution. It may be helpful for all to agree on trying one solution only for a set period of time.

....

Procrastination

Since I write a lot of books, people around me think that I'm immune to procrastination, just as it might appear from the outside that my house repels clutter. Neither could be further from the truth. I battle these problems same as everyone else. Procrastination and attention are a particular bane of mine. As with the techniques for clearing physical clutter, the only way to confront procrastination is turning to your list of the most valuable aspects of your life and deciding which pastimes fit into those categories and which do not.

Think carefully about what you throw out here. For example, I spend a lot of excess time surfing the Internet.

However, one valuable thing in my life is recreation. What sorts of time-wasting activities should I allow in my recreation? I decided that things like games are important because they support my love of play. However, spending too much time on snarky blogs or news sites makes my worldview more negative, and doesn't fit into the sort of carefree and rejuvenating recreation I envisioned for myself. Therefore, I quit reading those blogs and dedicated the time I would have spent reading them on my work and spending time with my family, since those were also valuable things for me.

If you find yourself procrastinating too much, you might have to get serious with yourself and set a schedule for recreation and work, giving yourself specific amounts of time for each activity. I like to start with the most difficult or dreaded project first. Just as it's a good idea to eat the tastiest food on your plate first, it's better to start with the activity that makes you feel more accomplished. Don't load up on empty time-fillers. Start earlier in the day with your most valuable projects, even if you're traditionally a night person. Make your priorities...your priority!

Perfectionism

Although it may not seem that way, people who hoard or collect more things than they need are perfectionists. Each item piling up represents a piece of the puzzle that is an ideal life; a life that is never quite lived. Perhaps a broken radio represents a dream of fixing something useful. A musical instrument abandoned on a shelf can seem like the potential to be a free-spirited musician. Likewise, the mental clutter of a perfectionist can be an odd assortment of obligations and paradoxical avoidance of some duties. If the perfectionist can't have it all, he or she will settle for nothing.

Relinquishing perfectionism is a tall order. For some it may begin with accepting constructive criticism. For others, it may help to think of themselves as a friend. Perfectionists are hardly ever as strict and harsh with friends as they are with themselves. Step outside of yourself and imagine what advice you would give to a friend who came to you with the troubles you have now.

For me, my perfectionism comes out strongest in academia. As an only child, I was encouraged to have the best grades possible. In fact, I was rewarded monetarily depending on what grades I achieved, with a bonus for perfect grades. This extrinsic motivation made me determined but nervous. In my head, I connected my parents' love and approval with the payout amount. One day, halfway through a quarter of college schooling, I found myself on the edge of an impossible and self-imposed dilemma. If I excelled, fine. If I didn't get perfect grades, I would drop out because I was struggling and not doing as well as I would have liked or expected of myself. Thankfully, I found another option: I told my parents that I had outgrown their reward system and that I would keep my grades to myself from that point on. My parents were bewildered, as even imperfect grades used to earn me cash, though not the "jackpot" of perfection.

To beat the clutter that perfectionism makes in your life, try practicing "good enough." Assess your anxiety level first in the same way you would if trying to let go of treasured objects. If you feel like you would lose your mind if you made an average grade on a paper or slacked off when painting the interior of your house, by all means move on to something that makes you less neurotic. Perhaps cutting corners on a recipe or ignoring a messed-up stitch when knitting a sweater is more your speed for now. I know that our house started getting clean when I quit trying to do top-to-bottom deep cleaning and settled for frequent but relatively half-assed cleaning.

Breaking Habits

I'm sure you already know what your bad habits are. Clearing clutter from your mental life may mean tackling some of your vices and bad habits head on. This may be incredibly difficult if you're set in your ways for the same reason that trying for anxiety-inducing goals first is difficult. It may seem odd to try to dismantle habits that aren't necessarily bad, but such an exercise can gently expose you to the light anxiety associated with breaking any habit. With practice and added confidence, you will be ready to eliminate a bad habit that perhaps you've failed to overcome many times.

Breaking even benign habits can help open your world up to a freedom you haven't known and thus remove clutter from your mind. For example, imagine that you eat the same thing for lunch every day at the same restaurant next to your place of work. If you never break that habit, nothing bad will happen to you. But you might never discover amazing new dishes at more interesting restaurants and perhaps even make some new friends in the process. Worst of all, you might fall into a rut in another area of your life. You might take the same route and the same stairs to get to that restaurant. The rut in your life might take on a ripple effect that makes routine feel like the only comfortable thing.

Challenge your habits and especially the bad ones (of course). It may be that you're already working on those. If you manage to eliminate one, good for you. But if you fail to quit a bad habit several times, try attacking a smaller daily habit. Change up what you buy at the grocery store. Buy a "challenge" ingredient to cook into a new meal. Teach yourself to do something long overdue, like how to swim, speak a new language, or ride a motorcycle. Take a bicycle to work instead of driving. Try a vegan diet. Anything that will break you out of your usual routine can bring you freedom from old habits and help you realize that you can change anything in your life at any time you wish.

You can replace your less stellar habits with good one. I can tell you that when I first started an exercise routine that included running, I *hated* it. But now, I can happily say that I have a positive addiction to running. Old habits can be broken and replaced with positive new ones that will energize and encourage you.

Relationships: Taking a Hard Look

Are your relationships in life valuable to you? There may be some relationships in your life that are not serving you in the way that they had in the past or should be now. Perhaps an adult son is draining your financial and emotional resources instead of setting off on his own. Or an ex-girlfriend may still insist on having you pick up her dry cleaning, even though you'd like to move on with your own life. Though it may seem cruel, you should take a hard look at those relationships and decide whether any pruning needs to be done. Setting healthy boundaries doesn't have to be a negative thing that makes you feel guilty. Be real with yourself. If you do have these types of relationships, chances are that deep down you know you aren't really getting back together with that ex or being a real help to your son. You'll have to be tough with yourself and clear those relationships from your life so you have room to breathe.

Even vital and necessary relationships can accumulate relationship clutter. Relationship clutter happens when the interactions between people become muddled with filler. Imagine coming home from work to a partner who immediately nags and berates you about the work you've neglected around the house. As a result, you might feel exhausted and negative about coming home after a hard day at work. The nagging might not be about anything important, and most relationship bickering isn't about the truly valuable things in life. Nevertheless, this relationship clutter can detract from shared values that could be enjoyed over a whole lifetime. Over time, this clutter can even undermine and destroy a relationship.

Many relationships get cluttered when one or both people in the relationship engage in mental accounting of things the other person does. This starts out with good intentions, as it indicates that a person has high expectations and is driven towards fairness and equality. The pervasive notion that people should always compromise in a relationship increases the feeling of being shorted if you do this mental accounting. In reality, each person has to go above and beyond the call of duty rather than meeting the other person halfway. It's only when you overlap your efforts that you can weave a strong relationship. You can't control the other person's actions, but you can set a good example and lead the way.

Getting Rid of Relationship Clutter

Again, nagging, bickering, snarky comments, and other relationship bad habits are things that will take time to prune out of your life and vocabulary. Start by imagining what you would like your interactions to be like. This is sort of like a visualization, only you may have to use all of your senses. Close your eyes and think about what perfect interactions with your partner would be like. Are you smiling at each other? Do you feel warm compassion for your partner as you talk? Are you touching each other or showing other signs of affection? Are you showing interest about each other's days and using active listening by making eye contact and asking curious questions?

As you move forward in your relationship, strive to make your interactions match your vision. You can initiate the sort of behavior you hope to see from your partner. It might be hard to change the whole pattern of your relationship all at once. You can try a day at a time, removing a little clutter at a time. For an entire day, for example, refrain from nagging and instead make it a point to recognize some good work your partner does and compliment that. On another day, instead of making a snarky put-down joke, say something to enhance your partner's self-esteem. You can decide whether or not it helps to let your partner in on your relationship improvement goals. You know your relationship best.

Eliminating Debt

Though it may not sound like it, debt is a form of mental clutter. Let me share with you an analogy I learned from my mother: Picture a rubber band ball. When you feel stressed and your life is full of clutter, it is as if your head is the core of this rubber band ball. Every rubber band taken off the rubber band ball reduces the amount of stress in your life. All the things you are supposed to do in life are rubber bands: calling and finally making a dentist appointment after months of stalling, paying a bill, getting your oil changed, and everything else. Major debts are many small and large rubber bands squeezing on your life, but every one you remove is a big burden released, even if it's just a small baby step toward debt freedom.

Some suggestions on eliminating debt include: credible counseling services, talking to your bank about consolidating or otherwise managing payments, getting a financial advisor, and creating a budget. Make sure to verify that any credit counseling or financial advisor professionals are licensed, well-reviewed, and have a good reputation with the Better Business Bureau. Creating a budget is beyond the scope of this book, but there are many fine books that outline a step-by-step process, and they can likely be found at your local library as well.

Working on your debt depends on your personal debt problem, of course. These are things you can discuss with a financial advisor. However, it is important to be aware of how seriously debt can clutter your mind. In American culture in particular, debt is socially accepted, and it's a way of life. But it may not be personally acceptable according to your own psychology. In such a case, having major debt can feel just as mentally cluttering as if you were not living in alignment with your values in any other facet of life.

e-clutter

Now that a "desktop" refers more commonly to pixels on a computer, virtual clutter has appeared along with it. Just as it is difficult to find an important piece of paper on a cluttered countertop, it is hard to find a valuable file on a computer in which nothing is organized and nothing is ever deleted. This virtual clutter represents mental clutter, because a crowded desktop and added minutes on your life when searching for an email are just as disruptive as physical clutter.

Sure, it may seem that one of the benefits of moving things to a computer is the lack of physical clutter. But virtual clutter can affect your life, so it is important to address the issue. Part of this may simply require organizing, like naming files and putting them in specific folders so you can find them quickly. Another strategy may be deleting excess photos or videos (especially blurry or mistake photos) to save space. Your strategy will have to meet your specific technological needs and limitations, so just remember that e-clutter should not be overlooked. Start by thinking about which areas of your virtual clutter may be affecting your life the most, and start deleting and setting an organization scheme in that area.

....

Clearing-Clutter Tip: Overhaul your email inbox. Be sure to route all your emails into one place and deal with them there. Don't use your inbox as a "to do" list by leaving emails in there to chatter at you.

Instead, sort through and deal with each email one by one, taking the time to unsubscribe from or filter the ones you no longer wish to receive.

Add something to your calendar or your "to do" list if you can't deal with it immediately. If you can, set yourself a half hour or an hour a day to check email and deal with messages so they aren't constantly distracting you.

....

The Chattering Monkey Mind

If you closed your eyes and tried to meditate at the beginning of this chapter, you probably encountered your monkey mind—the constant chattering that distracts you from experiencing the moment, your meditation, or simply from relaxing. The monkey mind might seem malevolent to some, telling you that what you are trying to do is stupid and that you will never be able to achieve true mental peace. For others, it might be a playful and cheerful distracting influence, encouraging you to check your Internet pastimes instead of paying attention to what's in front of you.

It is hard to defeat the monkey mind because it seems so constructive. Even the criticizing monkey mind might seem like it has some honest nuggets of information to share. However, be observant as to when the monkey mind presents itself. Even if it speaks the truth, the information may not be helpful to you if it comes in the middle of the night or when you are trying to concentrate on your work. Likewise, a playful mind is a good thing. However, playfulness at the total expense of any productivity can lead to more shame or discouragement than the joy that it brought in the first place.

The key to keeping your monkey mind from trashing your inner temple and creating mental clutter is to be deliberate about when you let the monkey run free. If you're creating a painting or writing a novel, this might be the perfect time to allow your inner narrative to run wild. However, if you're attempting to study for a final exam or to put the finishing touches on a major project at work, you'll need to be able to rein in your monkey mind. More importantly, if you're having a heart-to-heart talk with your spouse or child, you'll have to listen to him or her over the chatter of your monkey mind.

So how do you keep the monkey mind under control? You can't just cage it up and beat it. Treat it like a pet that you love but need to be obedient. Firstly, give it some freedom at designated times, maybe a creative outlet or a certain way that you play. Once you've got the care and feeding of your monkey mind down pat, you can try a little more training. If you haven't yet made daily meditation a routine, the potential escape of your monkey mind is a good reason to start. At first, it may seem nearly impossible to keep that monkey mind under control. You might have to ignore and release chattering thoughts with every breath you take for five miserable minutes. But over time and with practice, you'll find the process easier. With luck, you'll be able to attain freedom from your monkey mind whenever you want and for as long as you like. It is worth the gradual struggle to overcome the will of your monkey mind.

Stop Multitasking

When I was a small child, tests determined that I had Attention Deficit Hyperactivity Disorder. I always joke that I don't remember the testing because I wasn't paying attention. Later, I developed brain disabilities that made it even more difficult to stay on task. True attention problems are murderously difficult to deal with on a regular basis. As soon as you sit down to work on something, you are convinced that the project is impossible to finish. Your mind zips around like a hummingbird. If you let it, mental clutter can make it impossible to make real progress, so don't fall victim to that self-fulfilling prophecy. Your attention problems can be managed through careful scheduling and using the following tips.

One way to clear the clutter of your mind is to stop multitasking. While part of our culture these days, the human brain is still bad at multitasking. Even though the novelty of a new email message or checking a fresh screen feels satisfyingly motivating, it still takes time for your brain to switch gears every time you change tasks. If you split your tasks into several large chunks of time in a day, you'll accomplish much more work than if you gave partial attention to a larger project while occasionally working on other side tasks. The hard part is giving up those side tasks. The instant gratification of seeing something new when working on a tedious task feels amazing. Try telling yourself that single-minded work will allow you to complete all of your tasks sooner, giving you more freedom for what you want to be doing. Also, if you divide your tasks up by time on your daily planner, you can look forward to the light at the end of the tunnel at a specific time on the clock no matter what task needs to be accomplished.

How can you stop multitasking? Start by reducing the amount of time you allow for it. For example, spend several uninterrupted hours on your most important work when you arrive at work in the morning. After that, you can give time to some of your side tasks. If you really enjoy multitasking, you can allow yourself time to indulge. Reduce the changing of the gears as much as you can within a day. If you need, you can take baby steps toward this goal, such as turning off all distracting electronics when having family time, or even designating some areas of your house as electronics-free zones.

As the mother of two small children, I know that sometimes multitasking is absolutely necessary. There's no way I can work on this book while completely ignoring my babies. However, I can still work to keep the gear-switching to a minimum by lengthening the time I work between interruptions. That means no procrastinating after I've taken care of the babies and really have no excuse to delay sitting down at my desk and working. Even if you don't have the ideal amount of time available for the work at hand, you can still increase the amount of what you get done in a given day by resisting the pull of multitasking.

Most of all, though, if you truly suffer from attention problems, you'll have to learn to live with the grinding of those gears as you force yourself to get back on task. Sometimes I just can't avoid being pulled away from my work to deal with helping a baby or a preschooler. Of course I have visions of the perfect work space where I can write when I feel inspired and remain undisturbed, but the reality of my life is that this will never happen.

If I wait for those conditions, I will never get my work done. Instead, I've practiced until I have become an expert at resuming every task immediately after a disruption. It doesn't feel great. In fact, sometimes it feels positively painful. But not every chore feels wonderful all the way through, and mastering this particular skill can make your life feel more streamlined and less cluttered.

....

Clearing-Clutter Tip: A few hours before bedtime, power down all your electronic devices. Looking at the light from screens such as the television, computer, laptop, tablet, or even smartphone may actually make you feel wired and not ready to sleep.

Consider downloading a program or application that changes your screen lighting settings depending on the time of day, so your eyes gradually get reduced exposure to blue light, which is most associated with sleep disruption. Make this one small change to give you more restful nights.

....

The Here and Now

Sometimes the life of a dog or a small child is enviable. They live in the present without being haunted by past mistakes. They don't worry or plan endlessly about the future, and they don't even directly concern themselves with thoughts of death. This, essentially, is the complete lack of mental clutter—the ability to enjoy the present moment for what benefits it might have. A pleasant temperature, a satiated stomach, a feeling of health in the body, a dry place to take shelter; all of these exist in the "now." Before my father died, one of the last books he read was *The Power of Now* by Eckhart Tolle. Devastated by his passing, I quickly took the book to read for myself, since my mother said that it had received rave reviews. The embracing of the present moment seemed to be the message he tried to share with me in his last couple years of life. To a young adult daughter preoccupied with relationships, education, and career, he tried to describe the precious moment that is enjoying a cup of tea while overlooking a busy city street.

Living in the present moment is simple but incredibly difficult; you certainly can't let go of your future obligations. One solution is to release the way you beat yourself up over the past. Remember that concerns are things you can change, but worries should be relinquished if they are about things beyond your control. Relinquish all worries about your past. Forgive yourself for past wrongs you can no longer do anything more to right. If you've vowed to never do something bad again, offering whatever reparations and apologies are possible, you've done what you can and must move forward to get something good out of it.

Letting go of your future is not so simple. You can do it for moments at a time during meditation, but at other times it can seize you with (sometimes incredibly necessary) fear.

One strategy for reducing this pressure is to release attachments to outcomes, which you can read more about in the next chapter. Otherwise, you can simply work to expand the time you spend focusing on the present. Find time to be grateful for what you have and what you are experiencing in the present moment. Take time to notice the beauty of a sunrise or sunset. Take a moment with your child when he or she has an interesting question or catches your eye with an expression of love. Savor a bite of delicious food without immediately swallowing it to finish your meal. You may think you don't have enough hours in the day to appreciate the present moment, but the most exciting news about living in the here and now is that you always have time to just be yourself. Appreciate every moment as you live it. This isn't so much a switch you flip as it is a muscle you learn to use when you make everyday movements. Once you notice how it works, though, there's no turning back. You'll notice the beauty of a thunderstorm even when your bus is late on a rainy day.

"Every one of us has a special place in the Life Pattern. If you do not yet know clearly where you fit, I suggest that you try seeking it in receptive silence. I used to walk amid the beauties of nature, just receptive and silent, and wonderful insights would come to me. You begin to do your part in the Life Pattern by doing all the good things you feel motivated toward, even though they are just little good things at first. You give these priority in your life over all the superficial things that customarily clutter human lives."

....

Peace Pilgrim

Four

....

Spiritual Clutter:
Clutter Problems, Spiritual Solutions

In my training as an interfaith chaplain at the University of Washington, I learned some interesting things about the practice of spiritual care as it is practiced in hospitals throughout the country. As a religious person, I patted myself on the back when I learned that spiritual care for patients aids in the healing and recovery process. I was surprised, however, to find out which people have the worst outcomes after spiritual care. I learned that non-believers can pat themselves on the back, too, because those who believed they didn't have spiritual needs tend to fare as well as those who believe themselves spiritually rich. The ones who were more likely to have adverse outcomes or even die were those who felt spiritually conflicted, angry with God, or otherwise had a swirling vortex of clutter where the center of spiritual life is supposed to be.

It can be tough to be a spiritual or religious person in a secular society or in a community that values one form of religion above others. If you're not particularly religious but wish that there could be more ritual, spirit, or magic in your life, taking steps to rectify this problem can seem impossible. Our society presents a false dichotomy between the devout and the nonbelievers. In reality, there are many different colors in the beautiful rainbow of the spiritual experience. Even for religious people, the ideal spiritual life may seem too tall an order to fill. After all, there's always going to be some guru out there who seems to get more out of spirit than you do, so what's the point in trying? This chapter is about taking simple steps to reach the spiritual potential you were meant to find in this lifetime, rather than comparing yourself to anyone else's religious mission or agenda.

Some people may be content with only a few spiritual aspects in life. A cultural religious connection may be enough for some. Others may not be satisfied until they feel they've figured out the big question of what divinity is. For that reason, this chapter will be a collection of tips from which you can pick and choose. Your own appetite for spirit may change considerably once you start clearing clutter in the physical and mental realms of your life, and once all this time, space, and ability opens up, you'll have an opportunity to explore your spiritual needs. It is possible for spirituality to get too complex and cluttered with confusion to be fulfilling. This chapter is about finding your core spirituality no matter what your drive and desire so it can inform the other aspects of your life. With strong and cultivated spirit, your "need" for clutter in other areas of life can disappear forever.

Simplify, Harmonize, and Reflect Spiritually

To say that a complicated spiritual life has "too much" spirit would be misleading and, ironically, an oversimplification. Unlike the other realms of life, you won't need to remove any spirit from your life to simplify your spiritual life. What you can do is focus and refine your discipline to reduce confusion and spiritual discord. You'll find that seeking an ongoing harmony with your spiritual life and the other priorities in your life may be more difficult. It may be also a challenge to reflect on your spirituality in a meaning-ful way if you have no idea where you're going with this whole spirituality thing. Think of this cycle of simplifying, harmonizing, and reflection as a spiral. Each time you go around the circle, you may come to a greater understand-ing about what you want and need from your spiritual life. And of course, this is all about the journey more than the destination.

Step 1: Simplify

Check in and assess how much time and effort you are spending on spiritual understanding, growth, and fel-lowship. Are these efforts serving you well, or are you sim-ply trying to meet the expectations of family, a spouse, or an outdated self-image? If you've found yourself with too many religious obligations and have no sense of reward, giving up a practice that no longer serves you may help simplify things. Conversely, you may find a way to simplify your life by giving up something that conflicts with your religious or spiritual beliefs. It may be something simple like dietary restrictions or something complex like the way you think about your fellow human beings.

Try a thought experiment: Think about the resources you have because of your religion or spirituality. These might include a personal relationship with divinity, a connection with your culture or family, an understanding of your role in the world and how it works, comfort when encountering death, and so on. Now imagine that you had to give up one of those spiritual benefits. For example, you might want to give up knowing how the world works before you'd give up a connection with your god or gods. Now, continue the experiment by imagining another spiritual benefit taken away. Remember, you don't *actually* have to give these things up; the point is to appreciate what you have and get some sort of handle on your priorities. After reducing all spiritual benefits down to one you would never give up, you'll have some idea of where you need to focus your energy and daily practice to nurture your spirituality.

Remember, you don't truly have to give anything up if you feel you have what you need. Finding a focus or a touchstone of your religious practice is what will simplify your spiritual life. The more time spent doing what feeds your spirit most, the more your life will open up to other spiritual things that may orbit your central focus. If you're still having trouble figuring out what that focus should be, read the section entitled "Values" in this chapter.

Step 2. Harmonize

Seeking harmony in your spiritual life may be a challenge. Don't fall into an all-or-nothing approach; you don't have to sell all your things and become a bearded guru on a mountaintop to lead an ideal spiritual life. In fact, in some religions, like Wicca, it's important for spiritual leaders to be firmly grounded in a real and ordinary life. Balancing your mind, body, and spirit can happen when you take all three into account. Of course, when different stressors are happening at different points in your life, this balance will change. You'll know the balance is right when the harmony you find is able to act as a buffer against tragedy. When your life is out of balance and one little thing goes wrong, it will seem like *everything* is going wrong. Developing your spirituality and beefing it up to be in balance with your physical as well as mental and emotional needs in life will buffer you against devastation when change happens in any of those other realms.

To create harmony in your spiritual life, it may be important for you to find more ways to fill your life with spirituality. For some people, this may be as simple as bringing thankfulness into meals by saying grace or having a conversation with God at bedtime prayers. For others, this may mean exploring seriously what their religious faith tradition prescribes about lifestyle. Building moments into the day where you can check in with your deepest spiritual values can give you a constant in your life—nobody can take away from you. Harmonizing your spirituality with the other aspects of your life may mean expanding spirituality's place, too. That may mean setting time in your calendar or daily planner for meditation and prayer, or building time into your morning routine to record your dreams and connect with your higher self.

Step 3. Reflect

How do you feel about your spirituality and your relationship with the divine? Do you feel more comfortable in a box or a label, or are you happy without any labels for your spirituality? Are you at peace with your place in the spiritual world? Without this peace, might you end up one of those hospital patients suffering from a heartache where a God should be? You should consider how hungry you are for spiritual pursuits, and what drives that hunger. For example, some people never think about religion until somebody dies or until serious tragedy strikes. For such people, the scramble for religious support may be just another stressful thing to think about during a time of upheaval. If you are like this, it may be a priority for you to build a solid understanding about how your faith traditions can support you in times of need, before those desperate times actually happen.

For other people, the hunger for spirituality may come with a need for ritual and connection with family or culture. If you find a loneliness inside you that can only be resolved with fellowship, it may be your priority to find a group to fill your social spiritual needs. This process can take a long time. Finding a worship group can be a bit like getting married. There's a courting period during which you have to figure out whether you're a good fit for one another.

Finally, take a good hard look at any areas of contradiction you sense in your spiritual life. For most of us, this is obvious, like a teaching in your faith tradition you never could quite get behind. Or there may be some recommendation by your faith tradition that you support but simply can't seem to convince yourself is true or right for your life the way it is lived right now. Either way, it is important to address those discrepancies and figure out where you stand. And don't worry—doubt is a good thing. You'll either come back to your faith stronger than ever, or you'll find something even better for you.

Live Good Beliefs

A belief doesn't have to be only your understanding of the world. It can also be the understandings of the world you cherish or hold most dear to your heart. For example, it can be one thing to assume the best of people and to think that humans are inherently good. It is quite another thing to actively hope that people are inherently good and to place your faith in people on a daily basis. A leap of faith and action behind your hopes are both required.

Now is a perfect time for taking a good hard look at some of the reflections you've had about your spirituality. If, for example, charitable giving to the poor is a very big part of your personal beliefs and also a part of your faith tradition, it's time to align your beliefs with your actions. You don't have to take big steps that upend your life—try baby steps that bring you closer to your deepest values. To continue with the charitable giving example, you could begin a monthly volunteer date at a soup kitchen for the homeless or donate a small percentage of income to a charity whose values align with yours.

In most cases, we already have strong beliefs that inform our important actions such as voting, raising children, and choosing a place to work. However, even those important beliefs might be compromised as we deal with daily matters such as where we spend our money and what sort of hobbies we pursue in our free time. This is an opportunity to live your beliefs out loud. Find a cause you feel passionately about, and dedicate more of your time, effort, money or other resources toward a cause you have always valued.

Values

All throughout this book I've talked about values. When you wrote out some of your most valuable things in life, you were able to sort out your physical possessions to support some of those values. Those values may still apply to your spiritual life. For example, one of the most valu-able things in life is my family, so I endeavor to include my husband and children in my spiritual life. Some religious faith traditions may ascribe specific values you can name that won't fit necessarily into the more tangible physical valuables in life. Personally, my faith has specific values as I understand them: beauty, compassion, honor, humility, mirth, power, reverence, and strength. It can be helpful to distill your values into something you can reference on a frequent basis so your life won't get cluttered with things outside of your spiritual values.

For example, I decided to work with my children to come up with a family code of honor, which was basi-cally a big list of our family values strung together into a sort of sentence. We came up with a family motto/mission statement. Now, even when I am frustrated with my kids, I can look at that family mission statement and remember where my true heart resides. The family motto helps me if I'm about to do something emotional or physical that doesn't quite align with my values. I take a deep breath and try to do or say something that represents the best spiritual self I can be. There are many ways to be a good parent, and I try to simplify my life a little bit by focusing on those core values. This same sort of simplification can be used when relating to your work life, marriage, friend-ships, your favorite sport, or anything else.

Find Your Purpose

One thing all religions have in common is the idea that human life has a purpose, though your purpose here on earth may be different from the purpose of the person next to you. Finding your purpose is not really like getting a job; the idea is that you discover your place in the larger pattern of things as time moves on. Peace Pilgrim called this concept the "life pattern," and the idea is that we are all inextricably bound to one another. Humans—and indeed all living things in an ecosystem—are interconnected. If a purpose for the world exists, after all, we're all moving toward its goals together, like one massive organism. You might be the creature's hand, foot, or a vital organ.

Find out what makes your heart beat. It may be family life, a specific political cause, or a desire to act in service to others. Discovering your purpose can be a journey more than a destination. Still, it is an endeavor worth undertaking. And once you content yourself with a specific life purpose, don't fall into the trap of comparing yourself to others and feeling inadequate next to their life purposes. Self-satisfaction can lead to true happiness no matter what your station in life. Indian guru Sri Mata Amritanandamayi Devi (also known as Amma), wrote about this phenomenon in a book about living a simple life while taking care of a household. She pointed out that even rich Westerners who can afford things like air conditioning can be bitterly unhappy. However, a person who has nothing more than a hot and stuffy little place to call home can be filled with joy performing any action whether it is sweeping the floor or scrubbing the laundry, as long as the person makes every action a devotion to God.

Those of you who are very spiritually hungry or have a deep desire for religious connection will find another point of simplification when the focus turns away from the material and even the relational high points of life. Even when spiritual people fail at dreams of building a family or succeeding at a career, that person could be happy with a connection with the divine. Nobody can take that away. For some, simply turning one's focus to the divine can have the effect of taking the pressure off other areas of life. Sometimes we get what we truly want only after we stop needing it so desperately.

Ritual

Ritual and spirituality fit together hand in hand. There are many reasons for ritual's existence; it is a way to carve out a moment in time to make it special compared to others. Ritual can help put you in a spiritual headspace free of the everyday's mental clutter. Ritual can also link you to a simpler place and time, or to simple concepts that repeat themselves throughout history. Like a wheelbarrow wheel creating a rut in a dirt road, when the same ritual is performed over and over by many people, it seems to take on a life of its own. Over time, the ritual becomes easier and more effective. Even nonbelievers or very secular people can find themselves feeling a hunger for some sources of ritual to bookend the days. Here are a few rituals I believe can be helpful for you if you're trying to clear clutter from your life.

Saying grace before meals

A brief ritual before a meal can actually make the meal taste better. Saying grace before eating food can also help reduce body clutter; it causes you to be more mindful of what you are eating. Being thankful for the food that you eat can help you to empty your mind of envy or too many thoughts of the past or the future. Before you say grace, make sure to live in the present. If you have a candle on hand, light it. If not, simply say some words of thanksgiving. Holding hands around the table is one tradition that can help you feel closer if you eat together as a family. Here is an example of a grace prayer:

> In this moment, now, I'm thankful for food.
> I have all I need to help me feel good.
> I pray that I never know hunger nor thirst.
> And that I stop when my last bite is as good
> as the first.

Optionally, before anyone takes a bite, you can perform the ancient ritual of setting aside a bit of food for ancestors or any higher power you would like to include. You don't have to give much, just a tiny taste of whatever is on your plate. Offering food can be a symbolic gesture of laying aside seeds for planting in the next season so you will always be well fed and happy. Place these small offer-ings on a plate during the meal, and once you are finished, set the food outside for wild animals to eat in proxy for your ancestors or deity. Another option is to imagine that each bite you eat is an offering to your higher powers.

Prayer before bedtime

Establishing a ritual before bedtime can be very useful, act-ing as the key that opens the door to sleep. Essentially, you condition yourself over time to associate the act of sleep-ing with your ritual. You'll eventually find that sleep comes more swiftly if you always lay down after your familiar rit-ual. Any bedtime routine will do, but here's one I suggest: After you've made sure any chores that would keep you awake are complete, take a bath if you have the time. If you have lavender on hand, use it in the bath. If not, three pinches of salt and perhaps three drops of vanilla will do. Relax and meditate in the bath, allowing thoughts as they come to you to float away on the top of the water as if they don't belong to you. Say a prayer as the last thing you do before taking to your bed to sleep. An example of what you could say follows.

> Bless me while I close my eyes
> clear the clutter from my mind.
> Watch over where my body lies,
> bless this moment here in time.
> Guard me with protection steady,

health into my body streaming.
When I awake, let me be ready,
and remember that which I've been dreaming.

Hop into bed and make sure the prayer is the last thing you think about before you go to sleep. If you read in bed or chat with your spouse, be sure to do so before the prayer because you are working to condition yourself to fall asleep right after the prayer. If you believe in a higher power, you can imagine that you are laying your head in the lap of your beloved deity, in the same way that a child might rest his head in the lap of his mother. An alternative is to imagine installing your deity or deities seated in your heart where they reside through the night and day. Use the skills you practiced during meditation to dismiss thoughts other than the prayer after saying it. Meditation is also a great way to fall asleep at bedtime; it's usually a bummer to discover you've fallen asleep during daytime meditation!

Waking ritual

Like falling asleep with a ritual, waking up with one can be just the right thing for your body and mind once they become used to the routine. Undertake the ritual as soon as you shut off your alarm and get up for the day. If you're the type to hit the snooze button, don't start your waking ritual until you're actually getting up to start the day.

The first thing you do in this ritual is the prayer. Roll out of bed and touch the ground, which is a way to allow the energies of the dream world to exit your body. If you can, bow. If you believe in a higher power, imagine you are kneeling down to touch the feet of your higher power(s) as you pray and that you are placing them in your heart to be with you throughout the day.

> Bless me as I go about my day.
> Clear all clutter in my way.
> Give me all the joy I allow.
> Keep me in the here and now.

Next, move to the bathroom to take a shower. You may prefer to lay out your clothes the night before so as to not interfere with the ritual and to streamline your day. Step into the shower and take the time to meditate. You might wish to say prayers of blessings and protection at this time for people you love. You might wish to ask for intercessory prayer about things you find challenging. For example, a friend of mine prays every day for promptness, as she is often late for meetings. I pray every day that nothing pass my lips that does not first pass the three gates of speech: Is it true? Is it necessary? Is it kind?

After your shower, dress yourself while imagining you are putting on your values. Your shirt might be the value of humility, for example, and your belt might be strength and power. Match up each article of clothing to your own personal values so it's as if every day you put on a suit of armor to remind yourself that your true values are how you wish to present yourself to the world. If you use perfume, sunblock, or any other finishing touches, imagine that you are anointing yourself with divine blessings as the last thing before you exit your ritual to start your day.

Aromatherapy and Incense

Your sense of smell can be an excellent way to tap into your spirituality, and indeed, many religions use incense, anoint with scented oils, or otherwise use scented herbs in ritual. Why is the sense of smell so spiritually effective? It may be because scent is so closely tied to memory. The scent of baking cookies might instantly take you back in time to a moment spent in your grandmother's kitchen. Or, relaxation and other emotional reactions may arise from a simple scent and nothing more. These reasons may explain why scent is as yet another key to ritual. Incense and other scents are a way to condition yourself to have an emotional reaction or to get yourself in the right headspace for the activity you choose.

Having some incense on hand can help clear energetic clutter from the air as well as relax the body and mind, but don't clutter your home with a stash of incense you won't burn. If you have a charcoal incense burner, instead experiment with the herbs you have in your kitchen first. Here are a few common incense fragrances as well as some herbs you might already have on hand. Check the list and think about what you might want to make use of right now. Remember, since we're clearing clutter rather than gathering it, you shouldn't buy new incense unless you want to make immediate use of its influences in your home.

Cedar: Clears away negative energy clutter, purifies a space and lifts the energy of a space.

Cinnamon: May encourage visits from beneficial fairies that can help keep your home tidy.

Clary sage: Purifies a space and clarifies and energizes the thoughts of those therein.

Coconut: Good for relaxation and purification.

Copal: Clears away negative energies and spirits; calls in good energies and spirits.

Desert sage: Cleanses the energy of a space and raises peoples' energy.

Eucalyptus: Healing and purifying.

Frankincense: Clears away negative energy clutter and invites spiritual blessings.

Jasmine: May attract beneficial fairies who can help keep your home clean.

Lemon: Cleansing, purifying, and clears negativity.

Myrrh: Banishes negative energy from a space.

Peppermint: Clears the mind.

Pine: Purifies a space.

Rose: Clears a space of negativity, leaving pure love energy.

Spearmint: A gentle purification herb.

Sweetgrass: Blesses an area; raises peoples' energy.

Tangerine: Cleansing, purifying, and moves stagnant energy.

White sage: Clears away negative energy and energetic clutter of all kinds.

If you have more than one incense on hand, don't be afraid to make blends. For example, cedar, myrrh, and sandalwood blend together nicely to create a home purification incense. A simpler purification incense blend could be cinnamon and sandalwood. Burn a little bit as you mix the herbs together, because sometimes they smell much different when they're burning together, and you don't want to mix a large amount of incense and then discover that you don't like the smell once it is burning. Label your incense as you bag it so you don't misplace or mistake it for something else. Unfortunately, in the past I have created incense clutter myself with an excess of unlabeled bags—avoid my mistake!

You can also make oils for aromatherapy to use in a diffuser, to dress candles, or even to dab on yourself as a perfume if the oils won't irritate your skin. To make an aromatherapy blend, warm the oil up slightly on your stove and add the herbs. Stir in the herbs and then bottle them to steep for a time. In my experience, at least a month is good, from full moon to full moon. Turn and shake the bottle frequently to help the infusion process. Don't store the bottle somewhere where you will forget about it. I like to put the bottle on top of my tea container or near my bathroom supplies so I see it and shake it at least twice a day.

Once you've steeped the herbs long enough, strain the oil through some cheesecloth.

Sage smudging is a use of incense that deserves special mention. This is a cleansing and purification ritual that you can use any time you want to purify yourself spiritually, and metaphysically, it's more effective than a bath. To perform sage smudging, you'll need a bundle of white sage. Typically, white sage bundles are the size of a hand or bigger and tied with string. Keep in mind that you'll also need a safe place to set this bundle once it's burning. I like to use a large abalone shell filled with sand, and a stone or metal bowl will do as well. Sand adds a heat barrier to protect the surface on which you place the bowl. Make sure to place this makeshift incense burner on a surface like stone or brick, where you won't leave a burn mark.

Hold a lighter to the sage bundle and light as many tips as you can. Once they are lit, blow out the flame. You should see smoke billowing out from the sage bundle. (This is definitely not something to do in a room with smoke alarms.) At this point, you can hold the sage bundle in your hand if it is safe to do so, or you can place the sage in your incense burner. Either way, the ritual will work fine.

The next step is to waft the smoke all over your body. You can do this with a partner or on your own. Some people use a feather to waft the smoke to parts of the body. Others move the entire bundle of sage or the incense burner around to allow the smoke to reach all parts of the body. It is sort of like being in a reverse shower, where the smoke moves up instead of water falling down. "Wash" your body in the smoke and cleanse it of all negative energy. When you are done, let the sage bundle burn further if you enjoy the smell, or extinguish it in the sand and reuse it the next time you would like to clear clutter with the sage smudge.

Sage smudging can be incredibly useful in a new or cluttered space, as it gets rid of foreign or otherwise negative energies. Sage smudging can also be used on a daily basis. For example, a couple could smudge each other when they come home from work, each taking turns to talk about their day while the other does the smudging. This ritual could be done right outside the front door or in the garage. This way, the mental clutter of the work day is left behind when first entering the home. Sage smudging can also be added before any ritual, such as a bedtime ritual, to add extra clutter clearing energy.

Aura Cleansing

The aura is the halo of natural life energy or *chi* that surrounds every living thing (and perhaps many nonliving things as well). When you are feeling spiritually, emotionally, and physically well, your aura may become large, colorful, and vibrant to those who can sense auras. When you are feeling the clutter of life weighing down on you, your aura may also become cluttered. For those who can see auras, clutter may look like dark spots or have an overall dingy, faint, or constricted appearance.

Before you get started clearing your aura, you may wish to attempt to see auras. It might be easier to see the aura of someone else at first, since you live with yourself every day and are used to your own energy field, sort of like trying to identify your own scent. If you can get a partner, take turns viewing each other with a white wall as background. While you are being watched, concentrate on how you feel when you are trying to get a lot of attention. For example, imagine being on stage, passionately talking to a group of people about a topic that is important to you. This visualization may cause your aura to expand and become more visible. You can use this visualization while looking at yourself in the mirror if you are performing this experiment alone.

What does the aura look like? It may look like a colorful light, a fuzzy blurriness, or a wavy distortion in the background behind the body. If you can't see the aura, you might wish to reach out toward the skin to sense the aura. It may feel like warmth, a prickly sensation, a fuzziness, or just a sense of resistance, similar to the poles of magnets repelling one another.

The dark, dull, or constricted parts of an aura represent bits of clutter that have many different origins. Sometimes a cluttered aura can be a warning of illness or injury. And some people believe that clutter in an aura can appear around an area of the body that will soon be afflicted by some sort of malady. A cluttered aura can also indicate ailments more metaphorical in nature. For example, a dark spot at your throat might not simply predict a sore throat, but that you are not able to properly speak your mind. Clearing the clutter in your aura can balance out your life energy and allow you to act more freely with your spiritual efforts. Think of it as a spring cleaning for your body and spirit.

Sage smudging is an excellent way to clear clutter from your aura. Another traditional cleaning method involves passing an egg over your skin as if you were smudging with it instead of smoke. Cracking the egg afterwards releases any accumulated negative energy.

If you don't want to use incense or eggs, you can still clear the clutter of your aura. In fact, you don't need any extra tools at all. One way to clear aura clutter is by grounding, an energy practice that uses visualization to create a relaxed homeostasis where your life energy is neither drained nor amped up by your surroundings.

To perform spiritual grounding, first check in with your body to assess your current energy level. If you can see or feel auras, take note of any problems your aura seems to be indicating. Check in with your energy in other ways: Do you feel jittery, anxious, exhausted, or drained? Do you intuitively feel like you need more energy or less energy at this time?

Regardless of whether you feel like you need more energy or less, the first step is to rid yourself of excess energy. Don't worry, you'll always be able to replenish your life energy afterwards, and this cleansing process won't harm you no matter how low on energy you feel. Start by visualizing any excess or negative energy leaving your body through your feet. It may help to visualize yourself as a tree with roots that dig deep into the ground. These roots can even grow through cement floors and even the walls of apartment buildings, if necessary. Alternatively, you could imagine the energy as a flowing light traveling into the earth. It may help to remove shoes and socks to make a physical connection with the ground. Take a few deep breaths and hold this visualization until you feel yourself relaxing somewhat. Grounding takes experience to accomplish with precision, so you'll have to practice feeling what it's like when things are working well.

After you have grounded all of your negative or excess energy, the next stage is to draw up fresh, replenishing energy from the earth. Use the same visualization that worked for you, but in reverse. If you imagined yourself as a tree, visualize the tree drawing up nutrients and water from the earth. If you saw a light moving out of your body, see a new and refreshing light enter your body in the same way. Allow this visualization to move all throughout your body, paying special attention to any places where previously energy seemed to be stuck or having problems.

After you've completed your visualization, take time to check in with your energy again. If you can see or sense auras, take a good look. Objectively, how do you feel about your energy level? Ideally, you should feel relaxed and calm but alert. Grounding takes time to practice, so don't worry if you don't get the hang of it right away, or if it seems to take a long time. With practice, you'll be able to clear the clutter of your aura through grounding at a moment's notice, a vital skill if you have a particularly stressful job or family life. You might find that a lot of your stress will drain away more easily if you manage your spiritual clutter as it manifests in your aura.

Karma

What does karma have to do with attachment? In many Eastern spiritual traditions, everything! Most actions in life, good or bad, produce karma or attachment to our present world. Falling in love, starting a family, making an enemy, all these actions create attachments to the world in which we live. While attachment sounds like a wonderful part of living to some, to other spiritual traditions, these attachments are not such a great thing. Accumulated karma ties us to the world, and in some spiritual traditions, we become part of the cycle of death and rebirth, preventing us from the eternal freedom that is merging with the supreme divine nature of the universe.

The Western New Age version of karma simplifies the Eastern view considerably: one only needs to worry about bad karma, which encompasses actions that may cause harm such as being dishonest, hurting a friend, or stealing. These actions create a sort of soul clutter that can be cleared in this lifetime or the next. The more negative karma one accumulates, the more time must be spent clearing that karma instead of doing other fun things. Acts like helping the needy clear negative karma. The other way to clear it is a good old-fashioned attempt at making reparations and putting things right after doing something wrong.

So what's the point of karma? In terms of reincarnation, karma dictates the cycle of death and rebirth because the idea is that we are all born to learn specific lessons. When our life lessons are learned and the karmic clutter cleared, we can move forward. If the lessons aren't learned and the karmic clutter isn't cleared, however, we have to live a similar lifetime again and again (or perhaps an even worse one) to work on that backlog of clutter. I once visited a Vietnamese Buddhist temple to view some Buddhist relics and met some monks who had been reincarnated over many lifetimes simply, they said, to protect the holy objects. Now those were some people with simplified life plans and presumably no spiritual clutter! I also learned an interesting piece of lore from that particular sect of Buddhism (called Mahayana), that they consider karma a communal thing. In other words, karmic clutter is not just one person's clutter to bear, but many. They believe that none of us can move forward spiritually until all of us move forward together. Think of a giant traffic jam on the freeway during evening rush hour. Nobody can go home until everyone moves forward at the same time. You can see how this sect of Buddhism really encourages compassion for others and giving people a helping hand through life.

Outcomes and Letting Go of Expectations

Like me, you may have a hard time with the idea of releasing attachment. Another way to approach this may be to see it as letting go of expectations or attachments to outcomes, which was how I was able to understand the Eastern concept of attachment. I comprehend how harmful attachment was and how it could clutter up my mental and spiritual life.

You can compare releasing expectations to the process of cleaning a house, the repetitive drudgery you know by now. There's laundry to be done, a perpetually dirty floor, and dishes piling up with every meal. If you are attached to the outcome of a clean home, the constant "imperfection" can be quite disheartening. Now imagine you're the primary housekeeper for a busy family with young children and pets. Every time you clean the floor, your husband tracks more dirt in with his boots or the dogs run through the house leaving muddy paw prints. Every time you shop for groceries, you find a new thing your children won't eat. When you clean the dishes, you find empty milk glasses elsewhere that didn't make it to the sink. And even when your family tries very hard to do their respective parts to keep the house clean, mistakes are made. They add up and multiply for every additional member of the household.

If you were attached to the "clean house" outcome, you might even feel resentment toward your family members, even when they try their hardest. However, if you detach yourself from an outcome and simply live in the moment of your daily duty, you can find joy and release any feelings of resentment or being overwhelmed. You can sing while you work, laugh, talk with friends, and take pride in each task as it is done without want for the future.

How can you relinquish your attachment to outcome? Focus on the process rather than the outcome. In the house cleaning example, you could reframe your chore as a service to your family. Choose to experience love as you fold your beloved family's clothes. If you live alone, you can take pride in a mundane chore and in your mind inflate a sense of completion with each one. And everyone can add the spiritual component of performing each action in service to the divine. After all, taking care of your family or your environment serves to make the world a better place.

You can make your detachment to the material and attachment to the spiritual more overt by purposely turning cleaning house into acts of prayer. As you clean, say a mantra, meditate, or sing a hymn. You can also expand this attitude to other acts: clearing clutter, raising children, working at your job, or traveling from one place to another are all good times to pray. Over time, your life will feel more free, because attachments will have been released. You'll find yourself better able to work under pressure and complete projects you've started.

From Confusion to Enlightenment

Enlightenment is another Eastern concept that represents freedom from attachments and desire, and a union with the divine. Think of it as the ultimate relinquishment of attachments to anything but deity, something that may sound excessive to our Western ears. Actually, enlightenment has only been achieved by a few people throughout history. I certainly have not achieved enlightenment. In my mind, desire is good, and it is good to yearn for things. I tell my children "it's good to yearn" every day when they beg for things they cannot have.

If it helps, you don't have to think of enlightenment as some unreasonable goal on your "to do" list. Instead, think of enlightenment as a positive eventuality, like a peaceful death. Remember the Mahayana Buddhist understanding, that cumulatively humanity is moving toward enlightenment together. To that end, fighting enlightenment is silly at best and spiritually harmful at worst. Working to end at least petty or harmful desires and attachments could be beneficial not only for yourself, but for all of humanity.

Compassion

Some believe that the highest expression of spirituality is compassion for others, but it's often easier said than done, because we are taught to judge others in order to protect ourselves from harm. When you see a news story about something horrible someone has done, your brain may automatically make assumptions to distance yourself from that person: "The person was crazy." "The person was evil." Many of us have an automatic reaction, assuming that the situation or circumstance could never happen to us to make you act in the same despicable way. Perhaps you hope the bad person will be punished.

The way of compassion is to assume that we are more similar than different. Terrible outcomes, such as criminal behavior, the misfortune of homelessness, or drug addiction can happen to any of us. Think how your life would have been different if you were born in less fortunate circumstances or were forced to choose between your life or the life of someone you care about and some unethical action.

Having compassion for others can be helpful on an immediate level. For example, having compassion for a screaming toddler can keep you from making the situation worse by yelling in frustration. Having compassion for a stressed-out spouse can keep you from picking a fight from which your relationship may not recover. On a greater scale, compassion for other people may motivate you to volunteer your time and efforts to save lives by becoming a lifeguard or handing out food and blankets to the homeless.

Many people believe that developing greater compassion is the key to achieving enlightenment or at least relieving yourself from the stress of hating and blaming others. How do you develop compassion for others? Step outside your social comfort zone. Make friends with elders and people of different religions and ethnicities. Offer to volunteer to help people less fortunate than you, like the mentally ill or those in domestic abuse shelters. Actively search for similarities, even when your brain is screaming at you to find differences out of fear of what could happen to you if your circumstances were different. Strive to see the good in others, and tell yourself what you like about other people. Even a person you might consider extremely annoying has some aspects that are admirable. Make yourself a personality trait treasure hunter, searching for the treasures in every human being that you meet.

Give Up Feelings of Separation

These days, we separate ourselves from others more so than in any time in history. We may not even know the names of our neighbors. Social media and other electronic means of communication give us the illusion of closeness while simultaneously isolating us from our friends and relatives. A sad example from my own life is watching as two of my childhood friends developed dangerous eating disorders. I've seen their profile pictures on social networks shrink to skeletal levels but have felt powerless to do anything, since I never see them in real life nor speak to them on a daily basis. When I finally said something to one of them in a public forum online, he replied I was the first person to say anything and expressed surprise that he could literally skeletonize himself in front of the world without anyone seeming to care. I doubt that *nobody* cared. In fact, I think everybody in his extended social network cared and cares very much about him. But I think the illusion of separation discouraged people from speaking up.

Oddly enough, this same feeling of separateness can happen in real life as well. Crowds of people can stand by while someone is getting hurt right in front of them. In another personal experience, I was mugged when I fell ill at a very large festival surrounded by thousands of people. It was precisely because of the crowds that no one stepped forward to stop what happened to me. Now, I don't think that the bystanders who refused to help me were bad people; I think they were stuck in a world where they believed that helping me wasn't their problem and could potentially cause more problems for them if they overstepped their boundaries.

Perhaps the world would be a better place if we were each to take on the role of a personal superhero. We could clear the clutter of confusion and regret from our lives by having compassion for others and giving up our sense of isolation and our illusion that everything is "somebody else's problem." This goes back to my earlier assertion that most of the spiritual improvements you can make you already know you should make. You don't have to come to some new and fantastic revelation; you simply need to take on a new sense of responsibility for and dedication to beliefs that you've already held, perhaps your whole life.

You'll need to take a combination approach with techniques you've already seen before in this book. First, stop when you find yourself unnecessarily distancing yourself from others. Replace the thoughts that lead to that behavior with a script that agrees with your true beliefs, perhaps that you like something about others or that you have more similarities than differences. Combine these techniques with volunteerism to connect with the people you might otherwise avoid. For example, a friend of mine volunteered in the burn ward of a local hospital, because she was afraid of deformity. She learned to love the smiling faces of children even when they were healing from tragic burns. One of my own children was fearful of elderly people, so I started volunteering with my kids at a nursing home so they could make friends with a dynamic and wonderful old man who dispelled their fears. Confront your own fears and obliterate the illusions of separateness.

Letting Go of Selfishness

Letting go of selfishness is a pretty tough one for me. Every living being is programmed to selfishly protect his or her own life in order to stay alive long enough to reproduce, and overcoming this natural and biological urge is a pretty tall order. If you have family to call your own, start by letting go of selfishness within the boundaries of your own extended family. Helping your household helps yourself, after all.

Moving beyond the home environment is tougher. If you've struggled with feelings of separateness, you might think that letting go of selfishness is next to impossible. Don't beat yourself up about being selfish. That will just clutter your mind with guilt and negativity and, like I said, selfishness is a natural part of being alive. Instead, capitalize on your selfishness. Teach yourself to obliterate the boundaries of separateness by finding ways to help people who are similar to you.

For example, if you've suffered poverty in the past, reach out to help the impoverished. If you've suffered mental illness, reach out first to the mentally ill. Find people you can identify with and celebrate the small victories of unselfish action that result. Reach out with your strengths. If you already enjoy running, try going on a few charity or fundraising races whose causes you support. If you like building furniture, volunteer to put furniture together for the disabled. The idea is to gradually apply pressure to your comfort zone to expand your compassion, rather than throwing yourself out into strange situations and getting burned out on charity and volunteering before you get a chance to do any real good.

Peace

Now that you've worked hard to identify with others who are strangers to you, you might be feeling a deeper sense that peace should prevail on earth instead of war, death, and strife. However, aside from meditation, what can a person realistically do to promote peace? It starts within every person. You can take an action that might have a big effect, such as writing to your legislators about ideas for your home state or the entire nation that could bring about peace. Or you could do a small act that could still make a big difference, like a small change that could create more peaceful interactions with family, friends, and strangers.

Seek inner peace first. Through meditation and carefully clearing of all forms of clutter from your life, you can find a deep well of spiritual peace inside you, even if you're a naturally anxious or combative person. I'm an assertive person myself, and I never shy away from conflict, even when it's pointless inner conflict. To deal with this, I found that in any situation I could say the following mantra in my mind: I can choose peace instead of this. If I'm on an airplane holding a screaming baby while everybody gives me the evil eye, I think, "I can choose peace instead of this." If I'm arguing with my husband late at night when we both really should be getting some sleep, I say my mantra in my mind: I can choose peace instead of this. And when I'm just hungry and cranky, mentally willing a line to move faster so I can be done with whatever errand, the mantra always comes to my aid: I can choose peace instead of this.

Once you find inner peace, try to share it with those around you. Give somebody a smile who looks caught in his or her own turmoil. Let an argument go and just enjoy your partner or roommate instead of getting caught up in a pointless pattern of conflict. Relax and share a compassionate offer of help the next time that you see a mother struggling with a screaming child. Offer practical help or some healthy food to somebody who is struggling with illness or a life tragedy.

Once you and those closest to you are peaceful and free of drama, you can reach out to radiate peace further. Take political action if you like, or simply find ways to offer practical support for your peaceful goals. Offer to volunteer to help those who are suffering through conflict. Learn nonviolent communication and offer to mediate disputes between friends or family members. Become a beacon of peace wherever you go.

You don't have to force anyone to act like you, and in fact, doing that would be counter to the whole idea of peace. Instead, be so amazing that others will want to know your secret and be willing to lay down barriers and prejudices to be like you.

Prayer, Faith, and Trust

As your life becomes clutter free, you'll need to find faith inside yourself that everything you truly need will be available to you at the moment you need it. Otherwise you'll start hoarding things you don't need, be they clothes, more belongings, the habit of comparing yourself to others, or negative worries about the future and past. Having faith doesn't necessarily require being religious; the only faith you really need is the trust that you have everything you need. In fact, such faith is vital for a happy existence lived without fear. You'll have to develop trust in something: the divine, the general positive nature of the universe, other people, or yourself and your own resourcefulness.

One tool for developing faith in the divine is to develop a habit of frequent prayer. In this context, prayer acts as a constant conscious connection with the divine, the source of all good things you need. Think of it as having a direct telephone line to parents who love you and have set up a trust fund you can use any time. The point of developing a prayerful life is the ability to make that direct call any time you have a want or need. That way, you won't need to build up a soothing security blanket of physical or mental clutter.

The tough part about having a prayerful life is that you can't use a standard prayer, like the bedtime prayer I outlined on pages 157–158. You'll have to open up and engage in a conversation with the divine. With that in mind, what follows is some formatting advice.

Maybe you're sitting at home reading this book, or maybe you're in an airplane. You could be standing in a crowded subway car or stealing furtive glances while finishing lunch at work or school. Regardless of your surroundings, emotional state, or amount of free time, the moment has come for a basic prayer. If you're surrounded by people or otherwise self-conscious, feel free to pray silently in your head. If you're alone, you're welcome to shout it out. The purpose of this basic format is to make up a prayer on the spot, really mean it, and feel good about the results. Take a wild stab at it, and if you feel confused, don't worry—a full explanation of all the prayer's bits and pieces follows. Ready or not, here you go.

A Basic Prayer

Hail, [Name of god(s) and/or goddess(es) or "Spirit" or "to the universe"],

You who is/are [list three positive attributes of higher power(s)], I praise you!

Thank you for [health/money/love other specific blessing for which you need to ask],

[NOW!/ by next month/another time limit],

With harm to none, and for the highest good of all, so mote it be.

In return, I offer you [my eternal gratitude/my love and devotion/other offering or sacrifice].

Blessed be. (Pause, take three deep breaths, and be silent and alert for a sign, answer, or any other physical sensation or mental feeling.)

Give yourself a pat on the back for being brave enough to recite a basic, highly formulated though unscripted prayer. If you stumbled through it, that's because you had to make it up on the spot from only this outline. Notice which parts, if any, in the prayer slowed you down or made you feel uncertain, because those are the components you should give your serious spiritual contemplation.

Prayer components

The prayer has exactly seven lines. Why? Seven is a number of spiritual mystery in Pythagorean numerology and each line in this prayer represents an important component for both the beginner and the seasoned "veteran" returning to the fundamentals of prayer. You can remember the seven components to prayer through the mnemonic device PRAYING, which stands for: Person listening, Raise praise, Ask for help, Your deadline, Imperatives for safety, Note of thanks, and Gracious attention.

Person listening

Address the higher powers you are praying to by name as a way to get their attention and show your respect. If you don't have their names, you can use titles such as "God" or "Christ." If you are unsure of the nature of deity, you may address prayers simply to "Spirit," and if you are agnostic, you may direct prayers to your higher self or to the universe.

Raise praise

Since the beginning of time, people have propitiated deities through praise and worship. Think of these higher powers as loving parents to whom joyful praise brings a happy and beneficent mood. Likewise, focusing on the positive can help you nurture an optimistic outlook that will make you notice future blessings. Some people even believe that without due worship, their deity or religious tradition may not continue to exist and endure.

Ask for help

After you have named the divine respectfully and given your praise and worship, you can now request intercession in your life. It is okay to ask for help to either gain blessings or cleansing, but try to think beyond the process. Focus on the results you need regardless of how they will come about. For example, instead of praying to get the specific job you've applied for, thank the divine for the abundant wealth in the universe that is yours to claim, enjoy, and share. Instead of praying for a broken leg to mend well enough to bear weight for physical therapy, visualize yourself already running and jumping while you pray for continued physical health and healing.

Your deadline

Some believe that the divine operates on a very different timeline than we do. If you're praying for love and you receive it three decades after your prayer, you may have wished your prayer was answered more quickly. Likewise, you might state an end date to avoid too much of a good thing. Praying to find love, again, might backfire if you were hoping for monogamous marriage and instead find a new lover every week for the rest of your life. I find that it's helpful in many cases to ask for your prayer to come to pass by the next full moon or month. You can also ask for immediate intercession to be completed instantaneously, when necessary.

Imperatives for safety

In ancient times, many people believed the gods were tricksters, but prayers often still have little caveats for safety, such as "with harm to none" included in the words. This may be as much a reminder to the person praying the prayer to act mindfully as it is a sweet request to the divine.

Note of thanks

Giving and taking are necessary and beautiful parts in nature, life, and spirituality. To receive blessings from the divine, it's wise to offer a sacrifice. As a vegetarian myself, I don't recommend the practice of blood sacrifice of animals, and indeed many religions shun unwilling blood sacrifice of any kind. A sacrifice can be a physical offering of food, drink, flowers, incense, or anything else you value. Likewise, a metaphorical sacrifice can be made of gratitude, love, a promise to begin volunteer service, a vow of kindness, or any other intangible gift.

Gracious attention

All dialogue requires that each individual take turns speaking and listening. After you have spoken to the divine, you must take time to be silent and contemplative in order to perceive a reply if one is given. Attention can be paid through keeping a prayer journal as well as through silent and receptive meditation.

Attitude of Gratitude

Thanksgiving is an important component of prayer. A friend of mine saw her daughter find a lucky penny on the ground. She told her daughter to say a quick prayer of thanks, explaining that perhaps the divine doesn't know the difference between giving a little and giving a lot, so we should always be thankful. Later that day, her daughter found a five dollar bill on the ground. "She's sold on *that* one," my friend said. Giving thanks frequently to the divine, to those around you, and simply to yourself, can help you become a more positive person. It may also help you attract more positivity into your life. Gratitude can have a delightful snowball effect.

Say thanks whenever a prayer is granted. Say thanks whenever a blessing seems to come from nowhere. Say thanks whenever disaster is averted, and when you arrive somewhere on time safely and without incident. If you have a hard time catching those moments of opportunity to be thankful, you can build thanksgiving into your morning, mealtime, and bedtime routines. Then you will have at least three more times to be thankful each day than usual. When I'm going through an especially difficult time in life, I like to write in a journal and only include things for which I am thankful, allowing the negativity of the day to be forgotten. Some days are so hard that I might only have one or two little moments of thanksgiving written down, like gratitude for a good cup of tea in the morning. But, over time, I gather up gratitude and forget the bad stuff. Soon, I become a hunter of good things, looking all day for something to write in my journal. It's a good way to live, and it clears the clutter of negativity from my mind.

"When you have simplified your life, I'm sure you will feel as free as I feel. If your motive is one of giving then you will be given whatever you need."

....

Peace Pilgrim

Five

Other People's Clutter

Having a loved one who struggles with serious clutter problems can be devastating. If you have to live or work with such a person, it can be frustrating to have another person's stuff encroaching on your space. And even if you don't live with the person, it can be sad if they refuse to host your visits or if you simply don't feel comfortable around all that clutter. You might even see how a cluttered environment makes them feel confused, frustrated, and disorganized.

Naturally, you'll want to reach out to help, but getting people out of their clutter can be fraught with difficulty. The person you want to help could feel insulted or pressured and push you away. Even if your help is accepted gladly, you may find the process maddening. One person's trash is another person's treasure, after all, and you may find that the person simply has too many "treasures" where you see only trash. Even if you meet with some degree of success after everything is said and done, the clutter may simply accumulate again; all your hard work could be for nothing.

There are many reasons why helping others clear clutter is a delicate situation and one that should be approached carefully and in stages.

Gaining Perspective

A sense of perspective will be needed both for you and the person you are offering help. First, take a look at the problem as if you were looking at it from the outside. If the person is close to you, like a child, spouse, or roommate, consider your own reactions objectively. This way, your own frustrations can be solved independently. Since you already know how the clutter is affecting your own emotions, take a look at how it may be affecting your loved one. Is he or she unhappy because of the clutter? Are there problems finding lost objects or using the available space in the home as it is intended? Is the situation a fire or health hazard, or could it be problematic for small children who might visit?

Remember that giving your loved one a sense of perspective could be very difficult; that person may have spent years habituating to the clutter. What may be shocking and uncomfortable to you could be familiar to them.

You may need to reach out for some help from mutual friends to help your loved one understand that the clutter is affecting more than one person. Keep in mind that your intervention should above all be gentle. Ask curious questions and be dedicated to helping your loved one solve the problems he or she sees. Try asking, "Help me understand. What is the most challenging thing about clearing clutter for you?" Remember that giving up possessions can make people anxious, and the person might lash out if it appears you are using a threatening or accusatory tone. Try to collaborate and problem solve while politely ignoring any excuses that don't make sense.

Use "I" messages to make the problem about you and not your loved one. Here's a sample "I" message format. "I feel _____ when [your clutter affects me in the following ways]: _____. Please help me by _____." For example, "I feel anxious when we are late because you can't find your car keys. Please help me by clearing the clutter on the countertop and finding a permanent place for your car keys." Or, "I feel sad when I can't visit you during the holidays because your beds are too covered with clutter to have guests. Please help me by clearing space for me to sleep." Or, "I feel angry when I bring your grandchildren to the house and there are dangerous things on the floor that could harm them. Please help me by clearing the clutter and childproofing your home so we can feel safe enough to visit."

Teaching others to simplify, harmonize, and reflect

It may help to show the first chapter of this book to your loved one before you get started so that he or she knows what you're doing. Somebody who has always lived a cluttered life may have no idea what the constant cycle of housekeeping looks like. Don't get frustrated if the solution seems obvious to you. Your loved one may have never seen the process of clearing clutter in action in a way that was positive and fully within his or her control.

Step 1. Teaching others to simplify

Of course, the first simplification phase is going to be the most challenging. As a result, try to take baby steps and go slowly, allowing your loved one to have as much control over the process as possible. Be there to help by being the brawn for lifting and the brains for prompting. Be the driver of the car that will take things immediately to the dump and to a charity drop-off point. Help guide your loved one by asking questions like "Do you have a purpose for this object right now, today?," "Do you have a permanent place for this object right now?," "Have you used this object in the last six months?," and "Who else could use this more than you?" If you run across something the person is "saving" for somebody else, ask who it is for and when it will be given, and arrange for it to move as quickly as possible from the home.

If you run into opposition when trying to throw away something broken or something you think is clearly garbage, have compassion: your loved one is probably feeling a lot of anxiety right now. You can ask him or her to rate their anxiety at getting rid of the object on a scale of one to ten. Guide him or her to walk around the house and select something with a much lower anxiety rating to throw away. Remember that this process of gradual exposure to anxiety will have to be repeated many different times on many different occasions.

Don't let your loved one get burned out on the first cycle of simplifying. After successfully facing a mild to moderate level of anxiety by getting rid of something, back off and let the person take some time to harmonize and reflect before starting the simplification process again. By moving through the cycle, your loved one can begin to trust that the emotions that come up will resolve themselves.

Step 2. Teaching others to harmonize

Encourage your loved one to focus on other things after the first simplification cycle is complete. Perhaps there are intellectual, creative, or spiritual projects that have been left undone. These distractions will help to balance out a life that may have been previously focused on material clutter. This is also a good time to get mutual friends on board with the clutter clearing plan and encourage them to give experiences instead of stuff to your loved one for holidays and other occasions.

If housecleaning is something new to your loved one, be explicit with instructions on how cleaning the home should be accomplished. When I was learning how to clean my home after clearing clutter, my best friend put together a schedule of which rooms to clean on which days (like the one in chapter 2,) and I am forever indebted to her for making it. Customize a weekly schedule for your loved one's home and demonstrate what cleaning each room looks like. Your loved one might not realize, for example, that washing windows and dusting baseboards are a regular part of cleaning a room. Whenever possible, demonstrate with concrete examples and do the work together. House-work can be such an isolated task these days; it really is more enjoyable in cultures where several households join together to laugh and chat as they go about their chores.

Step 3. Teaching others to reflect

Set aside a time to reflect about the clearing process so you aren't just asking these questions in a nagging sort of way. Your loved one won't want to talk about clearing clutter all the time, after all. And during the process, it may be difficult to find some perspective in the swirling anxiety being experienced. Ask questions like: "What part of the simplification process was easiest for you?," "What was most challenging?," "What could make this easier in the future?," and "Do you have any ideas for how we can streamline any household chores and make them easier to do on a regular basis?" Collaborate together and set up another date to get started on the next simplification cycle and start the process all over again. After a time, you can certainly allow the process to guide itself. At first, however, think of it like teaching somebody to ride a bike. Allow the person to brace and lean on you for balance as long as you can take it and as long as he or she wants the help.

Shared Living

Anger can rise more quickly to the surface if you're teaching how to clear clutter to someone in your own home. If your loved one is not living up to your expectations, it can be tempting to apply pressure or give ultimatums you're not actually ready to carry out. Hold on tightly to your compassion and try to work with your loved ones to help them better themselves. As long as they are improving, catch them doing well and give encouragement.

Spouse

A spouse who seems to enjoy clutter can be the pits for someone who enjoys a more minimalist lifestyle. There will be some degree of going above and beyond the call of duty when cleaning up after your spouse, and perhaps allowing your spouse to do more for you in some other area of life. However, the two of you can still collaborate on ways to make life easier. You can also set some boundaries. Perhaps an area of the house or a part of the bedroom can be your space, and in those areas you can keep things clutter-free. Overall, you're going to have to use a lot of "I" messages with a cluttered spouse, if my experience is anything to go by.

Kids

Children's lives are getting more and more cluttered. Not only are their bedrooms cluttered with more toys than they need or use, their schedules can be cluttered with programmed activities too. Children may have no natural sense of order, so you will have to be very explicit when teaching them about clearing clutter. Try using photographs to show what an area looks like before and after clearing clutter. Teach your kids how to identify cluttered surroundings. When bringing a new toy home, ask your child to choose a permanent place for it, and whether there's a toy he or she could give away to make room for the new one. You may want to consider enforcing a "one in, one out" rule, and schedule regular opportunities for charitable giving. I like to have my kids clear out clutter on Thanksgiving to make room for the upcoming holiday gifts that are sure to come; it's also as a way to practice being thankful for what we have, need, and use.

The gift of boredom

If your children are struggling with an excess of programmed activities, consider scaling down on extracurricular sports and other classes. Kids who only play in organized teams or activities run by adults may not learn some of the problem-solving skills between peers that can be very useful later in life. Allow your children to bicker and solve their own problems, and teach them the skills they can use to ask questions and find solutions rather than always only enforcing your own solution.

If your children are bored, enlist them to help with housecleaning. Ask if they want to take a nap. Encourage creative thinking: tell them that something to do is right around the corner. If you sound like a broken record when they're bored, they are less likely to find reason to persist in trying to make you entertain them. Encourage them to spend time outside in nature finding new and interesting things to see and do.

....

Clearing-Clutter Tip: Simplify your kids' toy displays. Having too many toys out all at once gives the illusion of choice, but makes it less likely that they will play with any one thing for some time.

Place most of the toys in storage, and rotate a few displayed beautifully. Do the same with books so that only a few books are well read and then rotated out.

....

Roommates

Aside from finding a new one, a roommate who lives with a lot of clutter can be a tough problem to solve. You'll need to set more firm boundaries than you would with a spouse, and you'll need to do less teaching than you would with a child. Use "I" messages to zero in on the things that really bug you about your roommate's clutter. And of course, make plans to find a different living situation if you and your roommate are truly incompatible.

Elders

Some people only develop clutter habits in their old age, due to new anxiety thresholds built over a lifetime or mobility issues. It may be hard for an elderly person to accept that he or she can't manage the sort of housekeeping done in the past. Encourage the elderly loved one to visualize what he or she would like the golden years of retirement to look like. The new vision of the future can't look like life used to look in the days when work or family were more important. Work together on making the vision come true, and help your elderly loved one make decisions about downsizing his or her living space and acquiring help if necessary. You may be able to access local resources in your community that can provide volunteers for the elderly who need light housekeeping help.

Office Clutter

Physical office clutter can severely add to mental clutter. To see how that works, imagine you receive a memo about a report you need to give your boss on Monday. If you leave that memo in your line of sight, every time you pass it, a little voice in your head will say, "Don't forget to do that report!" If you have dozens of such reminders posted on the walls, stuffed in bins, or lying around, those piles of paper will all be chattering at you at once. Instead, as soon as a paper hits your hand, you should file it, add the information to your calendar, or do the work, if it is practical. And don't keep old calendars, as it's said that old calendars invite the negativity of the past year back into your life. Burn or recycle them to start anew.

....

Clearing–Clutter Tip: If you need to keep paper files of daily work, all you need is a total of forty-three files. That's thirty-one files for the days of the month and twelve files for the months of the year.

In your current working month, after you organize the work for each day, you just need to pull the new day's file at the end of each work day.

Don't forget to put work in files that are labeled a few days prior to the deadline, so that you have time to do the work.

....

Remember that your office space is never quite *your* space completely. Even if you don't mind a little clutter, your coworkers may, and keep in mind that when you move on to a new career, somebody will come in to replace you. If all of your duties and organization systems are in your head, there's no way for anyone to pick up where you left off. All the information you're keeping in your head also becomes mental clutter for you. Do your company and yourself a favor by keeping well-labeled and managed systems for how your job is done.

....

Clearing–Clutter Tip: When filing, always place the new contribution toward the back of the file, instead of switching between the back and the front or stuffing it in the middle. That way, you'll have a consistent and chronological order to your files.

....

Liquidizing an Estate

When somebody with a lot of clutter dies, the clearing problem is passed on to the next of kin, tasked with the burden of liquidizing the estate. If the deceased named an executor or an executrix, this person will be the primary person selling things and portioning out money to any named inheritors. Choosing an executor for your estate is a very important task. You may wish to choose somebody who is not extremely close to you, because the grieving person could feel terribly overwhelmed with that task right after your death. I've also seen many situations in which a hoarder was given the job of executor for an estate. Sadly, that dragged out the process of clearing the estate's clutter because the hoarder was unable to let go of the deceased's belongings, even if it technically did not belong to him.

If you have been tasked with liquidizing an estate, it is important to go through the duty as faithfully as possible. Even if you are reeling with emotions after the death of someone you know, the job of clearing the clutter and converting the assets into cash is clear. It may seem cruel to go through the task without emotion, but it is necessary. Your firm but gentle hand on the tiller, so to speak, will be appreciated once the turmoil of fresh grief is over.

Serious Problems, Help, and Resources

This book would not be complete without addressing the very serious problem of pathological hoarding. Clutter collecting is on a continuum, and there's no set point at which clutter becomes hoarding. However, you should recognize whether your clutter problem goes beyond the issues a mere book can cure. If your clutter is causing neglected areas of your home to suffer structural damage such as mold or termites, you have more than clutter. If pets or people are suffering health problems because of mold or when a pet can become inaccessible in the clutter, you have a serious problem on your hands. If there is an uncontrolled pest problem, waste is unable to be cleaned up, or you are in danger of losing your home because of bad housekeeping. You will need to reach out for help.

If you can afford the services of a professional organizer, they may be able to manage your problem before it causes any further harm to your life. If you can access health care, reach out to your primary doctor and ask for a referral to a therapist who can help you with your hoarding problem. If all else fails, you may need to call the police and ask for a referral to a safe shelter if you believe your immediate safety is in danger due to the conditions in your home.

Helping an Overwhelmed Loved One

If you see a loved one suffering from hoarding to the degree described above, it is important to intervene and try to help. If you are unable to help, or if he or she is not willing to accept help, you can access local resources for assistance. If a person is a danger to themselves or others through hoarding or is gravely disabled to the point where he or she cannot control clutter at a safe level, you may have to call the proper authorities to help. You may be reluctant, but it's not your job to dig someone out from their cluttered world. If called, the police may summon a county- or state-designated mental health practitioner who can help with hospitalization for psychiatric problems if necessary. Like me, you may not be qualified to diagnose such things, so you'll have to delegate when situations become too hard to handle on your own.

Conclusion

Clearing clutter from life feels like crawling out of a dark and constricted cave into fresh air on a bright and sunny mountaintop. If you allow it, even the smallest triumph can be a source of pride. You can sit back and relax overlooking a freshly mown lawn and weeded garden. You can cross your arms and admire a shiny, clean sink and clear countertop before bedtime. Watching a disordered shamble of sheets and blankets on the bed smooth out into a freshly made bed under your hands can give you a sense of power and accomplishment.

Carry the celebration of your discipline into the rest of your life. By clearing your mind of the clutter of things that don't matter, you can do things like finding your dream career, pursuing your creative callings, and enjoying the love in your life in the moments it comes to you. At the end of the day, and at the end of your lifetime, the clutter that orbited your life here and there won't matter. There's no sense in beating yourself up over a clutter problem you once had any more than there is a point to clinging to clutter when it will all be scattered to the four winds in a hundred years.

Play the following game with your kids or by yourself the next time you walk out your front door: Scan your surroundings for things that cannot be bought or stolen. These things might be a smile from a woman walking her dog on the sidewalk, or the smell of a spring rain. These instants of beauty and love in the world are what truly matter, so much so that people characterize these things as above and beyond the material world. Spirituality is what we call those missing puzzle pieces that truly fit into our lives, and in that spirit, I hope you will never find yourself wanting for anyone or anything.

Appendix

The International Obsessive Compulsive Disorder
Foundation: http://www.ocfoundation.org/
treatment_providers.aspx

National Crisis Hotline: 1-800-273-TALK (8255)

Bibliography

Babauta, Leo. *Zen Habits: Handbook for Life.* Seattle: CreateSpace Independent Publishing Platform, 2009.

Cunningham, Scott and David Harrington. *The Magical Household: Spells & Rituals for the Home.* St. Paul, MN: Llewellyn Publications, 1983.

Devi, Sri Mata Amritanandamayi. *Immortal Light: Advice to Householders.* Amritapuri, Kerala, India: Mata Amritanandamayi Mission Trust, 1994.

Payne, Kim J. and Lisa M. Ross. *Simplicity Parenting: Using the Extraordinary Power of Less to Raise Calmer, Happier, and More Secure Kids.* New York: Ballantine Books, 2009.

Pilgrim, Peace. *Peace Pilgrim: Her Life and Work in Her Own Words.* Santa Fe: Ocean Tree Books, 1992.

Stack, Laura. *Organizing Your Office and Your Life: Clear the Clutter and Your Mind*. Renton, WA: Audioink Publishing, 2012.

Stone, Melissa. *The Key to Life is … Balance: Weekly Om's to Help You Find Balance*. Felton, CA: Dragonfly Publishing Company, 2008.

Summers, Selena. *Feng Shui in 5 Minutes*. St. Paul, MN: Llewellyn Publications, 2002.

Tribole, Evelyn and Elyse Resch. *Intuitive Eating*. New York: St. Martin Press. 2012.

Walsh, Peter. *Enough Already!: Clearing Mental Clutter to Become the Best You*. New York: Free Press, 2009.

Webster, Richard. *101 Feng Shui Tips for Your Home*. St. Paul, MN: Llewellyn Publications, 1998.

———. *Feng Shui for Beginners: Successful Living by Design*. St. Paul, MN: Llewellyn Publications, 1997.

Whitehurst, Tess. *Magical Housekeeping: Simple Charms & Practical Tips for Creating a Harmonious Home*. Woodbury, MN: Llewellyn Publications, 2010.

Zasio, Robin. *The Hoarder in You: How to Live a Happier, Healthier, Uncluttered Life*. Emmaus, PA: Rodale Books, 2012.